FIGHT
AGAINST
TIME

BOOKS BY STEVEN CLARK

FIGHT AGAINST TIME

THE COMPLETE BOOK OF BASEBALL CARDS

ROLLER HOCKEY

FIGHT AGAINST TIME

Five Athletes—
A Legacy of Courage

STEVEN CLARK

New York
ATHENEUM
1979

Library of Congress Cataloging in Publication Data

Clark, Steven, 1951–
 Fight against time.
 CONTENTS: Introduction.—Freddie Steinmark.—
Danny Thompson. [etc.]
 1. Athletes—United States—Biography. 2. Cancer
—Biography. I. Title.
GV697.A1C597 1979   796'.092'2 [B]   78–20353
ISBN 0 689 10953 9

TO HOLLY ANTONOFF CLARK,

my wife, and very closest friend.

ACKNOWLEDGMENTS

IT CAN BE DIFFICULT, WRITING A BOOK SUCH AS THIS, TO find people willing to talk about those who were once close to them. Fortunately, I found a tremendous amount of cooperation among the many people I contacted from Boston to San Francisco, Minneapolis to Austin.

I greatly appreciate the assistance received from Mike White, Tom Roth, Paul Hackett, Jim Symington, Jack Miyamoto, Harold Zimman, Ted Lepcio, Buff Donelli, Marty Harrigan, Tony DeFilippo, Ben Schwartzwalder, Joe Szombathy, Father Fred Bomar, Spanky Stephens, Scott Henderson, Red Coats, Harmon Killebrew, Dave Goltz, Tony Oliva, Chet Bryan, and Mr. and Mrs. James Thompson.

I would also like to thank sports publicists Ed Carpenter of Boston University, Larry Kimball of Syracuse University and Tom Mee of the Minnesota Twins. Much thanks to my good friends Doug Gould, who supplied information, Richard Rothschild, who provided some important facts, Norman Liss, who knew some of the right people, and Al Sperber, who provided some late inning relief.

This book could not have been written without the love and affection of my wife, Holly, and my parents, Anne and Benjamin Clark. Surely, this is the greatest help of all.

Steven Clark

INTRODUCTION

No ONE HAS EVER SAID THAT DEATH WAS FAIR, THAT dying was limited to the old and the weak, yet it is hard to justify the end of a young and powerful man, his vigor gone, his radiance extinguished. The death of any young person is a tragedy too great for words. And the death of an athlete seems to be the greatest anomaly of all.

It is the athlete who blooms earliest, who reaches his stardom years before the musician becomes fully accomplished and the businessman becomes wealthy. To many of us, the young athlete who graces the magazine cover and picture tube seems little less than immortal. So strong, so healthy, he could ward off affliction with a snap of his fingers.

Or so it would appear. What follows are the stories of five flesh-and-blood men who lost their fight against time, but who crammed an inordinate amount of courage and accomplishment into a brief lifetime. These were special men on and off the field, who left legacies for generations to follow. In playing, they caught the accolades of the crowd. In dying, they captured their hearts.

Ernie Davis was college football's premier running back in the early 1960s. A decade earlier, Harry Agganis thrilled the fans in Boston with his finesse in throwing a football and smacking a baseball. Joe Roth was an All-American quarterback and a surefire pro prospect. Danny Thompson was the Minnesota Twins' shortstop and inspiration. Freddie Steinmark was the little University of Texas defensive back with the giant heart.

A black kid from upstate New York. A Greek boy from the wrong side of the tracks in Boston. A golden-haired boy from the beaches of California. A farmboy from a tiny town in Oklahoma. A cop's son from a Denver suburb. Every one was different, yet in many ways so very much alike.

At least four of them knew they were dying, yet never burdened anyone with their fears. Each one worked hard to reach his goals, yet never forgot where he had come from. The nation put them on pedestals, yet they felt more comfortable with their feet on the ground.

"Really, just figure I'm a normal guy," said Joe Roth to newsmen who knew he was dying. "What if some guy sitting down there on the street corner got cancer? Would everybody make a big fuss?"

How does one mark courage? Is it simply knowing that one's days are short? Or is it being able to stare death down and live a full life to the very end? This takes guts, and these men showed it.

They displayed a tremendous amount of faith. While each struggled to survive, at the end each man was also strong enough to accept his fate. Yet while they lived, how they lived! They achieved greater recognition and success in twenty-odd years than most people achieve in seventy-five. Ernie Davis led Syracuse University to the national championship, won the Heisman Trophy and became the highest paid rookie in the National Football League, all by the age of twenty-two. Harry Agganis was an All-American football player at Boston University and the Boston Red Sox' first baseman by the time he was twenty-four. Joe Roth was considered the best college quarterback in the land at twenty-one. At twenty-three, Danny Thompson was called up by the Twins to help them win the pennant. Freddie Steinmark at twenty-one was an integral part of Texas' quest for No. 1 ranking.

The yardstick for measuring the impact of a man's life is to ask those who knew him best. Desire and courage and decency are the words that occur over and over again in discussions about these men.

"He represented the very best in young people," Father Fred Bomar, a parish priest, says of Freddie Steinmark. "I've told my people his life was a series of sermons. Not preaching, but by example."

His words would fit any of them. When Harry Agganis died, he was memorialized in every Greek Orthodox church in North and South America. The United States Senate curtailed business to pay tribute to Ernie Davis. The President of the United States kept close tabs on the progress of Freddie Steinmark.

Mostly, these men cared about others. They wanted people to feel good in their company. Self-pity or sympathy from others had no place in their lives.

"I know how much I can do for a lot of people, how much it will mean if I keep a positive attitude about the whole thing," said Joe Roth. "I know how much I have to be thankful for, how many right turns at the fork in the road I've been fortunate enough to make. I appreciate how much people care. In a way, it [the cancer] is a good problem to have."

Obviously, the speaker was more than just a man who could throw a football sixty yards. Like Ernie Davis, Harry Agganis, Danny Thompson and Freddie Steinmark, he was more than a word in a headline or a picture in a newspaper. For these reasons, as much as for their recorded achievements, they were five extraordinary men.

CONTENTS

FIGHT
AGAINST
TIME

FREDDIE STEINMARK

BRIAN PICCOLO, THE CHICAGO BEARS RUNNING BACK, agonized over the letter for days. He wrote it and rewrote it, wanting to make it perfect.

It was late January, 1970, two months after Piccolo had had a malignant tumor scraped from his chest, and he was on the way to recovery, or so he thought. Now he wanted to express his feelings and hopes to another young football player who was in a Houston hospital recuperating from the cancer surgery that had cost him a leg.

"Joy, I have to write him," Piccolo explained to his wife. "I just wish I knew what to tell him."

From the fall of 1968 through December 6, 1969, Freddie Joe Steinmark had started every game on defense for the University of Texas Longhorns, the top team in the nation. Even on that December day, he had played virtually every minute that Southwest Conference–rival Arkansas had had the ball. The game was for the conference title, a trip to the Cotton Bowl and the national championship, and Steinmark's team had won, 15 to 14.

Only one thing marred the jubilation of the post-game celebration—that aching left leg. Now that the Arkansas game was over, Freddie felt he could at last get it checked, but he wasn't prepared himself for the diagnosis: the pain came from a tumor in Freddie's thighbone. The next day, he was flown to Houston's J. D. Anderson Hospital and Tumor Institute and underwent exploratory surgery. A biopsy showed the tumor was malignant and the doctors operated without delay. Freddie Steinmark's leg was amputated at the hip.

The response was immediate and came from all across the nation. During the next six weeks, Freddie received hundreds of telephone calls and approximately twelve thousand pieces of mail. They came from politicians, athletes, friends, concerned people. But perhaps the one that meant the most to him came from Chicago on a winter day. It was from Brian Piccolo.

Dear Fred:

Although I don't know you personally, we have a lot in common. This is why I'm writing you this letter. My football career, just as yours, was brought to a sudden halt this year by cancer, mine in the form of a tumor located directly below my breastbone.

2

This tumor popped up from nothing to the size of a grapefruit in a period of about three months. I had my surgery on November 28 at Memorial Hospital in New York and missed the last five games of the season.

I watched your game against Arkansas from my hospital bed when I was recovering from surgery and then read about your problem a few days later. I guess that I, more than any other football player, know how you felt. I spent a lot of time thinking about you and praying for you in those days and that's when I decided I would write. I never got to it until Mike Pyle (a center with the Bears) visited my house when I got home from New York and informed me that you were a Bears fan. He found out through Don (Moon) Mullins of Houston, a former Bear.

Fred, I guess I'd mainly like to share with you my feelings since my operation, simply that our lives are in God's hands, just as they were before our illnesses were known. And I shall never stop praying to God for the strength to carry out the plans He has laid out for me.

I know you are a courageous young man and I hope this letter may be of some help to you. Perhaps some day we may meet one another. I'm sure we would have much to talk about.

Best of luck to you, Fred.

Your friend,
Brian Piccolo

3

Freddie treasured the letter and kept in touch with Piccolo. The two, however, never met.

On June 16, 1970, Brian Piccolo died from the spreading malignancy. Almost exactly one year later, on June 6, 1971, Freddie Joe Steinmark succumbed to the same disease.

Physically, Freddie Steinmark was a featherweight in a game of heavyweights. At barely 160 pounds, he looked more capable of riding a thoroughbred racehorse than dragging down a 220-pound fullback. His spirit and competitive nature, however, more than compensated for his lack of stature. As Darrell Royal, his coach at Texas, said, "When I first met him, I suspicioned he had 150 pounds of heart. My suspicions were correct."

Spanky Stephens was two years ahead of Freddie at the University of Texas. Now the team's trainer, he remembers the tiny defensive back as a man who closely followed the credo of Vince Lombardi. "Winning isn't everything," the Green Bay Packers' coach had said. "It's the only thing."

"He was quiet and real businesslike and a fierce competitor in everything he did," says Stephens, the Longhorns' student trainer during Freddie's playing days. "Whether it was football or cards, he would do anything to win. His goals were to do the best he could possibly do. For everything, he put his whole self into it."

Freddie was taught the importance of winning early from his father, a Denver police detective. Fred Steinmark, Freddie's dad, had been an exceptional high school athlete in Denver during the 1930s. Upon gradu-

4

ation, he had been given a small bonus to sign with the Cleveland Indians and had actually spent several years in the minor leagues with teams in Green Bay, Wisconsin, and Meridian, Mississippi, moving up the professional baseball ladder. Then a head-on collision with a coal truck nearly killed him. He fractured both legs and suffered numerous other injuries, and though, after several operations, he recovered sufficiently to play with the Enid, Oklahoma, team in the New York Yankee chain, the needs of his young wife, the former Gloria Marchetti, and his young son, Freddie, required his full attention. He was forced to relinquish his dream.

So the father groomed his oldest son to pursue the sports career he had given up. While the whole family—sisters Gloria (Gigi) and Paula Kay (P.K.) and brother Sammy, later a defensive back for the University of Wyoming—was intensively competitive on and off the field, it was Freddie who became his father's, and the family's, protegé. In later years, the entire clan traveled ten times from Denver to Austin—a twelve-hundred-mile round trip—to watch Freddie in action.

"Freddie was always very family-oriented," says Scott Henderson, a Longhorn linebacker and Freddie's closest friend at Texas. "He was always very protective of his sisters, anxious about his little brother and concerned about his parents. They were all very strong-willed people. The children were all given a good Catholic upbringing."

As a result of the family's sports enthusiasm, Freddie was wearing a baseball uniform around the house by the time he was two years old; by three, he was whipping a baseball around with his father; and at four, he was wearing a football helmet to dinner. His father would sit him in front of the television set on Sundays to watch the Chicago Bears, whose games were broadcast in Denver—the Bears were Freddie's favorite team until the Denver Broncos arrived—but the object was not to sit back and enjoy, his father said, but to learn the finer points of football.

Unlike many young athletes who are turned off by parental pressures, however, Freddie seemed to rise to the task. His father's scolding and criticism about how he fielded a grounder or carried a football drove Freddie to greater heights.

"But we would argue," Freddie wrote in his autobiography, *I Play to Win*. "I remember once after our team won a Young America game by 40–0, he jumped all over me about some goof I had made. Even after we won by 40–0! He'd yell at me, and sometimes we would both wind up crying. But I know what he was trying to do. He wanted me to do the things, wanted to teach me to do the things he always wanted to do himself, to keep me from making the mistakes he had made, to impress on me that I had to excel, that I had to go to college, that I had to get an education and, chances were, sports would be the only way we could afford it.

"Part of my drive to be a good athlete was because my parents and relatives all had such high hopes for me. They all took such great delight any time I played well. It was like a victory for the whole tribe. It was something I wanted for myself and it was also something that really

6

made them happy. So it was just a natural ambition for me."

In order for Freddie to get the full benefit of junior sports, his father arranged for him to play football and baseball with a local team called the Rough Riders, a conglomeration of no-nonsense coaches and tough kids from Denver's working-class neighborhoods. At the time, Freddie was all of seven years old and weighed fifty pounds. The team *was* rough, and the coaches did not condone mistakes, often swatting a player on the side of his helmet until he got it right—but Freddie usually got it right. In the eight years he played for the Rough Riders, the team won nearly every one of its games.

In school, Freddie's athletic prowess was not limited to football and baseball. As an eighth-grader at Manning Junior High School, for instance, he won the 116-pound wrestling championship and excelled at basketball, skiing, tumbling and swimming. But there was no doubt which sports he preferred, and it was at suburban Wheat Ridge High School that Freddie's abilities really began to shine. An infielder on the school's baseball team, he made all-conference three consecutive years, competed in the Suburban Denver All-Star Baseball Game, and upon graduation was drafted by the Cincinnati Reds, who even offered him a small bonus. Freddie toyed with the idea of playing baseball for a little while, but in the end, football was his first love.

It took awhile for him to star, though. In his junior year, he earned his way into the Wheat Ridge starting backfield, only to have an injury sideline him after four games. This was unusual. Injuries rarely stopped Freddie from playing. As a Rough Rider he had played with a broken arm, infected toenail and a badly inflamed big toe. This time, he even played one game with a broken bone in his right leg, but the doctor finally ended his season by putting him in a cast. "He had an extremely high tolerance for pain," Spanky Stephens remembers.

In 1966, Freddie's senior year, his situation changed for the better. John "Red" Coats was hired to coach the Wheat Ridge football team—the previous coach had been fired for his inability to beat arch-rival Lakewood. Football was big business in Denver.

Coats brought a new and exciting style with him. He changed the offense from the Wing-T to a more professional setup that allowed for more diversity, and instituted a tough, gritty, charge-ahead approach that appealed to players like Freddie.

"I first met Freddie during the spring when he was playing baseball," says Coats, who has recently retired as head football coach, but still assists the Wheat Ridge golf team. "I could tell immediately that he had a certain sense of what was happening. He was a real dedicated athlete, very intelligent and also very gifted." On a team that included Bobby Mitchell, later Freddie's roommate and an all-Southwest Conference (SWC) guard at Texas, and a half dozen other scholarship athletes, Coats called Freddie "our leader and the player we couldn't afford to lose." That year, the team chose him as one of its four captains.

At five feet eight inches and 152 pounds now, Freddie was playing in both the offensive and defensive backfields, and having a great year. The real test would come, however, when they met vaunted Lakewood. Both Wheat Ridge and Lakewood were rolling along unbeaten and untied when they met at the Jefferson County Stadium on October 7, 1966. Lakewood, the perennial Jefferson County League champion, entered the game with a string of twenty-four straight league victories. Although the stadium seated only about eight thousand fans, nearly eleven thousand crammed into the park that day, including the entire Steinmark and Marchetti clans.

For three periods, Lakewood and Wheat Ridge played each other to a standstill and they changed sides for the final period tied at 13–13. On the very first play of the fourth quarter, Freddie took a handoff from quarterback Roger Behler, popped through the middle of the line and raced down the sideline. Hemmed in, he suddenly cut back toward the middle of the field, waited for his blockers to regroup, then darted past the last remaining defenders to complete a thrilling seventy-seven-yard touchdown run. His game-breaking dash gave the Wheat Ridge Farmers a hard-earned 19–13 victory and a clear path to the state championship.

"It wasn't so much the seventy-yard run that beat us," said one player after the game, "as his eighteen unassisted tackles on defense."

Two months later, Wheat Ridge got by a tough George Washington team to win the Colorado AAA title for the first time in the school's history. Coats later led the Farmers to championships in 1967 and 1973 as the winning tradition continued.

On top of his athletic prowess, Freddie was also proving himself capable in the classroom. At the end of his senior year, he recorded a 3.64 grade point average out of a possible 4.0, and graduated twenty-fifth in a class of 530. His performance athletically and academically earned him the coveted Golden Helmet Award, given annually by the *Denver Post* to the top scholar-athlete in the state. At the same time, he was named the top prep athlete of the year by the Colorado Sports Hall of Fame. His future seemed assured.

But it wasn't that easy. Honors notwithstanding, Freddie was all but ignored by the major football schools. Unlike several of his teammates who were besieged by college offers, Freddie found himself forced to go out and sell himself. That winter he wrote to the head coaches at Notre Dame, Alabama, Duke, Purdue, Wyoming and Oklahoma. The returns were less than inspiring. He received a couple of form letters and several that said thanks, but no thanks. He knew why.

"It was strictly because of his size that he had trouble getting a scholarship," according to Coats. "He was Catholic and like most Catholic boys he wanted to go to Notre Dame. They weren't interested."

Even the University of Colorado at Boulder, which, like most state schools, grabbed up as much local talent as it could, showed little interest at first in Freddie. The only school that pursued him with any vigor was Dartmouth College of the academically rich, football-poor Ivy League. Coach Bob Blackman of Dartmouth was impressed both by Freddie's gridiron instincts and his classroom acumen and offered him a grant-in-aid schol-

10

arship which would have covered the cost of his entire education. Though Freddie was fond of Blackman and the school, he was not attracted to Dartmouth's sports program. Over the strong objections of his mother, who favored an Ivy League education, Freddie decided to hold out for a school with an athletic reputation.

Coats also believed that Freddie was capable of playing big-time football. He himself had attended Texas Tech, and he busied himself writing to schools throughout the southwest, extolling the virtues of his star running back. Finally, he got a nibble from Mike Campbell, the defensive coach at Texas, and, with his teammate Bobby Mitchell, Freddie was on his way to inspect, and be inspected at, the Austin campus.

On February 26, 1967, Freddie and Mitchell were met in Austin by several varsity football players and given a quick tour of the campus and the sixty-seven-thousand-seat Memorial Stadium. For Freddie, it was love at first sight.

The next day they met Darrell Royal, the Texas head coach with a reputation for churning out winning football teams. Freddie, a bit sensitive about his size, wore his high-heeled cowboy boots to the interview. Royal, who had played quarterback for the University of Oklahoma in the 1940s at 158 pounds, was not concerned about Freddie's appearance, however. He was familiar with Freddie's game clips and had sized him up carefully. Steinmark had the ability and the desire: that was all Royal cared about.

Although Colorado put on a last-minute blitz to land Freddie—after having treated him like some poor relation—the Wheat Ridge flash was set. He was heading, with Mitchell, to Austin.

At the Texas campus that summer Freddie was tremendously impressed with the precision with which Darrell Royal ran his troops through practice. Everything seemed perfect, from the scrimmages to the tackling drills to the attitudes displayed by coaches and players. Even the dormitory accommodations were carefully arranged to keep the athletes happy and motivated.

That summer, Freddie set his goals for himself. Like any college athlete, he hoped to make All-American. He also wanted to make the All-Academic team. He knew there were several players in the National Football League who were no bigger than he was and he wanted to be offered a professional contract. But most important —and more down to earth—he wanted to start every game as a varsity player.

In his first year, the freshman team went undefeated. Freddie—with Mitchell, the only out-of-state members on the team—started in the defensive secondary and played some wingback on offense. The next year, Freddie was listed as a fourth-string defensive halfback during spring practice with the varsity, but within two weeks, he was moved up to the second team. By the late summer practices, he had hurdled over Scooter Monzingo, a regular the previous year, into the starting lineup—the first player from his class to reach first-string status.

Freddie's first varsity game against the University of Houston was less auspicious, however. The Cougar team dominated the game from the outset and the Longhorns were lucky to escape with a tie—even though Freddie intercepted a pass late in the game that could have resulted in the winning touchdown.

In football, they say gaining a tie is like kissing your sister. If that's so, the Longhorns kissed the feet of the Red Raiders from Texas Tech the following Saturday. In the town of Lubbock, Texas, Royal and his players were ambushed 31–22 and left for the buzzards. The season looked gloomy indeed.

Then something called the wishbone formation changed everything around for Texas. The coaches decided that starting quarterback Bill Bradley was not built for the new run-oriented offense—he was moved to wide receiver and then to the secondary—and Royal brought in a flashy chance-taker named James Street to run the team. Suddenly, everything clicked. The victories started during the second week in October with Oklahoma State and ended thirty games later against Notre Dame in the 1971 Cotton Bowl.

At first, however, it seemed as if nothing had changed. Oklahoma, Texas' next opponent, was a tough team, and with 2:37 remaining in the game, Texas found itself trailing, 20–19. Then Freddie called for a fair catch at his own fifteen-yard line; Street threw three times to Daryl Comer for eighteen, twenty-one and thirteen yards; and Bradley caught one for ten yards. Two runs later, Texas hit paydirt for a 26–20 lead. There were thirty-nine seconds left.

Oklahoma quickly moved back upfield, reaching the Texas thirty-seven-yard line in only three plays. On the final play of the game, quarterback Bobby Warmack fired a pass into the Longhorn end zone. Several players went up for the ball, but it was Freddie Steinmark who came down with it as the final gun sounded.

The next week, in a tough conference battle with Arkansas, Freddie got his hands on another enemy pass to help the Longhorns hold on and win, 39–20. Hardly panting, Texas proceeded to steamroll its next five opponents—Rice, SMU, Baylor, TCU and Texas A&M— by the cumulative score of 205–82.

The Longhorns were just beginning to flex their muscles. In post-season play, the SWC champions met Tennessee in the 1969 Cotton Bowl game and proved to be rude hosts. Leading 28–0 by halftime, Texas went on to top the Volunteers, 36–13. The wire services placed late-blooming Texas No. 3 in the year-end polls behind two undefeated teams, Ohio State and Penn State.

In all, Freddie had gained 177 yards in twenty-five punt returns that season for an excellent eight-yard average—fourth best in the conference—and his five interceptions had given him the second highest total in the SWC. With a major in chemical engineering, he was also chosen for the All-Southwest Academic Team. In his junior year, he would be named an Honorable Mention All-American and a second team SWC choice by the *Dallas Times Herald.*

With the football season over, Freddie could at last relax, but relaxing did not come easy to him. If it wasn't football, it was studying, and Freddie worked hard, staying pretty much to himself. He often took in a movie with his high school girl friend, Linda Wheeler, who had enrolled with him at Texas, but though friendly with some of his teammates, he spent relatively little time with them away from the football field. As Father Fred Bomar, a priest at St. Peter the Apostle Church in Austin, and later a close friend of Freddie's, would say following his death, "His teammates really didn't get the chance to know him."

That summer of 1969, after his sophomore year, Freddie was working in a Denver tire store when he first began to feel a dull ache in his left leg. The pain got worse when the team reported for two-a-day practices on September 1. Freddie figured he had calcium deposits in his leg or, at worst, bone chips, and nursed the leg through much of the pre-season scrimmages, hoping the pain would disappear with the warm weather. It did not.

The smallest man on the starting team, Freddie had always had the reputation of a hustler during practice. He went all out in practices and treated wind sprints as if he were running qualifying heats in the Olympics. Now, however, he was suddenly going at less than full speed. His coaches were concerned, particularly Fred Akers, the secondary, and later head, coach. In games, Akers noticed, Freddie was not meeting the action as quickly as before and seemed to be conserving his energy on plays he realized he could not become involved in. That was unlike Freddie.

"I always had been taught, and truly believed, that you played in a game only as well as you practiced for it," Freddie later wrote. "Some guys maybe can loaf during the week and then turn it all on when the bands start playing on Saturday, but I've never believed in it for me. That's the reason I always tried everything with

15

all-out effort, even to the point of running every wind sprint just as hard as I could.

"Perhaps this all goes back to my size. I'm not the biggest guy in the world, of course, so I had to work a little harder to get the job done. You must make adjustments for any shortcomings you may have if you hope to compete with the best."

During the course of the 1969 season, Akers toyed with the idea of replacing Freddie with Rick Nabors, but decided to keep the winning combination—Danny Lester, Tommy Campbell and Freddie in the middle— intact.

Meanwhile, the people at ABC were hoping that their final television game of the season would pit against each other two teams competing for the national championship. Since they realized there was a good possibility that both Arkansas and Texas could go through the season undefeated, they asked the teams and the NCAA for permission to shift their game from October 19 to December 6. The permission was granted. The network execs sat down and prayed.

As the season progressed, it looked like their prayers were being answered. Both Texas and Arkansas marched through their seasons, Texas averaging more than forty-four points and 376 yards per game, and allowing only two of its opponents to score as many as seventeen points against it. At the same time the Arkansas Razorback defense was permitting a phenomenal average of less than a touchdown a game. The stage seemed set for an epic confrontation, but there was still Ohio State, No. 1 for eight straight weeks, to contend with. Unless the

Buckeyes lost, the Texas-Arkansas game would not be for the national championship.

Then, in their last regular season game, it happened. Ohio State fell to Michigan, 24–12—and ABC had its dream match. The ballyhoo that immediately inundated both campuses quickly spread to the rest of the nation, and even to the White House itself. The week before the big game, President Richard Nixon announced he would personally attend the game and award a plaque to the winning team.

Big game or not, though, Freddie Steinmark was miserable for most of that week. For the first time, his left leg was hurting badly. The heat treatments applied by trainer Frank Medina helped somewhat, but Freddie was starting to get nervous. What if it wasn't just a case of calcium deposits? Medina wanted him to have the leg checked out immediately, and Freddie promised—but not until the Arkansas game was over. He was not going to miss *that* game for anything.

He had been limping on and off for several weeks now and his teammates were calling him Ratso, after the crippled con artist in the movie *Midnight Cowboy*. Freddie ignored them and prepared for the Arkansas game by staying in bed all week except for meals and football practice. He cut his classes and took Darvon, a prescription pain killer, at night so he could get enough sleep.

The Friday before the game, the Longhorns flew into Fayetteville, Arkansas, and spent much of the day working out on the Astroturf of Razorback Stadium. Freddie used ultrasound therapy and hot packs on his leg.

It is a well-known fact that the state of Arkansas lives and dies with its Razorbacks, and under the leadership of Coach Frank Broyles through the 1960s and much of the '70s, it's been mostly living. However, if there is one team that has consistently given it trouble, that is Texas. In a sport known for its bitter rivalries, the competition between these two teams is perhaps the most intense, and on December 6, 1969, the evidence of it was everywhere. Razorback diehards, dressed in red clothing, roamed the crowd, calling out their piercing "Soooooie piggggg!" cry, while Texas fans responded vigorously with the "hook 'em horns" sign: a slight alteration of the "okay sign," whereby the middle fingers and the thumb of the right hand form a circle while the index finger and pinky are held aloft.

Both sides had to wait until President Nixon arrived by helicopter from Fort Smith, Arkansas, and was escorted to his seat on the fifty-yard line. Then the game began.

Both teams experienced some early jitters. On the second play of the game, Texas fumbled and Arkansas recovered on the Texas 22. Five plays later, halfback Bill Burnett bulled ahead six yards for the first touchdown. By the fourth period, the count had reached 14–0 in Arkansas' favor. Texas simply could not keep its hands on the ball: four fumbles, two interceptions . . . cries of "Soooooie piggggg" filled the stadium.

Then, on the opening play of the final quarter, Texas' James Street rolled out looking for tight end Randy Peschel. Unable to locate him in the Arkansas secondary, he tucked the ball under his arm and sprinted forty-two yards for the Longhorns' first score. On the next play, keeping the ball himself, he dived across the goal line for the two-point conversion. Suddenly it was 14–8 and things looked a bit brighter for the few Texas rooters.

But Arkansas was not about to lie down. They roared back into Texas territory, and with the ball resting on the Texas twenty-yard line, quarterback Bill Montgomery faded back and spotted receiver Chuck Dicus with several steps on Freddie. Freddie saw the ball coming and knew he had to think fast. He was hopelessly beaten on the play and Dicus was about to catch the ball and go in for the touchdown that would give Arkansas an all-but-unbeatable 21–8 advantage. There was only one thing to do. Freddie reached out and held Dicus and prevented him from reaching the ball. A penalty flag went down immediately and Arkansas was awarded a first-and-goal-to-go on the Texas 10. But they hadn't scored yet. Now they would have to earn the touchdown.

They could not. On the very next play, Freddie's defense held and Longhorn safety Danny Lester intercepted Montgomery's pass in the end zone. It was the turning point of the game. Texas came back with a brilliant series of plays to take the lead, 15–14, with less than five minutes to play, and again the Texas defense held Arkansas scoreless as the seconds ticked by. With only 1:39 left, Bill Montgomery threw up another pass—and it floated down into the Longhorns' arms. The Razorbacks' championship hopes abruptly evaporated.

Minutes later, President Nixon entered the bedlam of the Texas locker room to shake hands with Coach Darrell Royal and members of the Longhorn team and officially crowned Texas the national collegiate football champion before millions of television fans. He got into a bit of trouble over it: Joe Paterno's Penn State team was also undefeated and untied and considered by some the top club in the country. Pennsylvania Governor Raymond Shafer even went so far later as to extract a public apology from the President. But none of that made any difference to Freddie and his teammates that day. Their team was No. 1. Arriving back home in Austin, they were mobbed by students and fans at the airport. That night Freddie drank beer for the first time ever—after all, it was against training rules—and smoked a cigar at the gala celebration. Victory was sweet.

More than a hundred sportswriters from around the country had nudged their way that day into the Fayetteville press box. Millions more had watched the game on television. During a time of vigorous American protest, and disenchantment with the war, it was a football game in a college town of twenty-seven thousand in Arkansas that had grabbed the limelight.

"They played for the college football championship of the universe in this suburb of Dogpatch Saturday before the President of the Yew-nited States of America, Billy Graham, God, Governor Rockefeller and 44,000 people, all of whom had shoes and hats with no bullet holes in them," wrote Jim Murray of the *Los Angeles Times*. "The President showed up late, but Texas almost didn't make the game at all. They slept through the first three quarters. Then they scored 15 points in 14 minutes and, all over Arkansas, guys in squirrel hats went out and kicked the dog or slammed the cat's tail in the door.

20

"The game was played in a rotting old stadium first erected by the WPA and while the stands were filled with 40,000 Lum N' Abners and a few thousand oilmen in orange boots, the hills outside were filled with ever-lovin' peaceniks. But Fayetteville achieved an eminence it hasn't known since the whole town hid in a cave from General Grant. They ain't ever going to believe it back in the hills. The President of the whole Yew-nited States . . . woo, sooie pig!"

Now, however, Freddie had to keep his promise. The Arkansas game was over, and that leg would have to be checked. The Sunday after the game, Freddie and Linda went to a 5:00 P.M. mass at the Catholic Student Center and he told her he would see a doctor Monday. The next day technicians at the Student Health Center took X-rays of Freddie's throbbing left leg, and that night, while he and Linda attended a Longhorn basketball game, the doctor gave him the preliminary news—it looked like a bone tumor. Freddie was shocked.

"It was like a physical collision with something in the dark," he wrote later. "A truck just rammed me in the stomach. It wasn't cold that night; I was wearing blue jeans and a shirt, but in a matter of seconds, I was soaking wet. I got this terrible taste in my mouth. Bone chips, yes. A strained knee, even that good old calcium deposit, okay. But a bone tumor?"

That night, after he had dropped Linda off at her dormitory, he went to the Catholic Student Center to pray and cry. He knew the implications of a bone tumor. Later, he called his father in Denver.

The next morning, further X-rays confirmed the ear-

21

lier pictures. There was a clear spot about the size of a golf ball sitting in the thighbone, right above the kneecap. The doctors decided to fly Freddie immediately to the J. D. Anderson Hospital and Tumor Institute in Houston for further observation.

Returning to the dormitory to pick up his gear, he ran into his friend Spanky Stephens, the team's student trainer. They talked for several minutes before Freddie was driven to the airport. "It was just after the draft lottery and he had gotten a real high number like 355 and I had 77," Stephens recalls. "He told me he knew there was a chance he might never play sports any more, much less march in the army. He said he wished he could change numbers with me."

Darrell Royal was in New York City with co-captains Ted Koy, James Street and Glen Halsell at the National Football Hall of Fame banquet at the Waldorf Astoria Hotel when he heard the news. He immediately flew to Houston.

"I was up there accepting the MacArthur Bowl and riding on cloud nine when I got the telephone call," Royal said at the time. "He's got a tubful of guts, that's all I can say."

Freddie's family came in from Denver and his closest friends on the team, Scott Henderson and Bobby Mitchell, drove in from Austin with his girl friend, Linda.

Freddie got the straight story as soon as he walked into the cancer institute. There was the possibility, chief surgeon Dr. Richard Martin told him, that what he had was a blood clot, osteomyelitis or any one of a number of other things. If it was a tumor, it might even be benign,

he said. Chances were, however, that it was malignant—
and the leg would have to be amputated.

Father Fred Bomar called Freddie on Thursday as
soon as he heard about the tumor. Father Bomar knew
him only slightly at the time, but was an avid Longhorn
fan and the priest at the church where several Texas
football players regularly worshipped. "He asked me if
I would come down," Father Bomar recalls now, "so I
drove down and sat with him and his parents the day
before surgery."

That night, understandably, was a tense one. The
strain had been hard on Gloria Steinmark, Freddie's
mother, who several months before had been hospitalized herself and undergone several transfusions for her
bleeding ulcers. Together, Father Bomar and Freddie re-
cited the *Memorare*—a prayer for assistance under
trying circumstances. Combined with some sleeping
pills, it seemed to help. The patient had a restful night.

Early Friday morning, Freddie was wheeled out of
room 415-W and down to the operating room. The tumor
was extracted and tested. It was cancerous. There was
no choice; there could be no delay. The entire leg was
removed.

The wire services immediately got wind of the story,
and before long, Freddie's room was piled high with
flowers, candies, cookies and letters. He was given a
personal secretary—later two—to keep up with his in-
coming calls and mail.

But that Saturday, he answered few of them. He was
under sedation most of the day, though he did stay awake
long enough to see the Liberty Bowl on television—won

by Colorado, 47–33 over Alabama—and greet several members of his family. The following day, he picked up the telephone and found himself talking to the President of the United States.

Coach Darrell Royal was a close friend of Bud Wilkinson, the ex-Oklahoma football coach who was then in charge of the nation's physical fitness program, and he had asked Wilkinson to relay the news of Freddie's operation to the President. The call had been the President's immediate response.

He spoke to Freddie for fifteen minutes that day. He would talk to him several more times in the course of the next eighteen months.

"It picked my boy up quite a bit," said Freddie's father afterward. "I'm sure he gave him quite a pep talk. He greatly admired the boy . . . admired his courage. He's getting along quite well now. He's taking it like a champ, a lot better than I can take it."

The statement released from the hospital was succinct. "This type of malignancy is called bone sarcoma," it read. "It originates within the bone itself. Bone sarcoma gives no evidence of its presence until it either grows outside the shaft of the bone, forming a bulge, or causes pain."

Football had had no effect on the growth of the tumor. The result would have been the same no matter what Freddie had done or been. The fortunate thing was that the bone—which is susceptible to breakage in this state —had not been fractured during the season. A broken bone would have allowed the cancerous cells to spread quickly, leaving Freddie no chance of survival.

24

The outpouring of warmth and support from across the nation was staggering. The University of Texas football team sent Freddie flowers, orange carnations forming the words "No. 1." The Rice team sent a telegram that read, "To an outstanding and great person. We want you to know in this trying time for you that all of us are on the same side of the scrimmage line." The Oakland Raiders, champions of the American Football League, sent him their championship game ball. He received television sets, radios and stereos. A wealthy alumnus commissioned an artist to do an oil painting of him. A Freddie Steinmark Trust Fund was started and money poured in.

And he received letters, thousands of them, not only from men like Brian Piccolo, but from ordinary people who had themselves suffered similar setbacks. One was from a high school athlete named David Fusco, who had recently undergone the same operation.

"Nobody had ever heard of David Fusco and his high school football career and his operation just like mine," Freddie wrote later. "He didn't have a special secretary just to handle the calls. Did somebody send him a color TV, did the President call him? And yet, there was David Fusco sending me a letter of sympathy."

It was all very new to him. Suddenly he was getting attention he would never have received as a nameless member of the No. 1 college football team.

During his stay in the hospital, Freddie took the time to talk with other young people who had gone through the same thing he had. He realized there were ten thousand David Fuscos out there to one Freddie Steinmark—

young men and women who would never get national exposure.

Meanwhile, the doctors at J. D. Anderson told Freddie that, as far as they knew, he was clean of the cancer—but there were no guarantees until at least five years had passed. Freddie knew the odds.

"He had a dogged determination to live," says Father Bomar. "We both knew what the odds were after the surgery. I demanded the same attitude of myself that I demanded of him. One of determination and hope and optimism, not one of despair."

Brought up with a strong belief in God, Freddie did not go through the post-operative depression that many amputees suffer. While in school he had attended mass three days a week and on Sundays at the Catholic Student Center. He had prayed on his knees before falling to sleep each night. He had said two rosaries before every football game. His faith was intact.

"I'm just sorry it [football] had to end," he told a reporter for the *Houston Post* shortly after the surgery. "But sometimes good things come to an end. I just thank the good Lord that He gave me the chance to come down here and play. I even enjoyed going to practice every day. You never realize what something means to you till you don't have it anymore.

"I was looking forward to playing Notre Dame in the Cotton Bowl. I won't get a chance to play, but I'm happy my teammates will play. Even when I was a little kid I always dreamed about playing Notre Dame one day."

Two days before Christmas, Freddie held a press conference in the Astrodome. He walked with the aid of

26

aluminum crutches clasped around his wrists, and sat in a gold chair as he watched the $2 million scoreboard explode as it usually did only after a touchdown or a home run. This time it spelled out the words, "The Astrodome salutes Freddie Steinmark—the No. 1 team's No. 1 guy."

"I feel real thankful," Freddie told the reporters. "The doctors have given me a lot of hope. They've always leveled with me . . . I don't look upon it as a defeat in any way. I knew what the chances were before the surgery. They said there was a real good chance I would lose my leg. They never pulled any punches."

Freddie then said that he planned to be on the sidelines with his teammates on New Year's Day in the Cotton Bowl—and walking with his artificial leg by the January 12 lettermen's banquet in Austin.

He knew this would take some doing. He was just beginning to gain back some of his weight after dropping to 128 pounds after the surgery. His new leg would be difficult to fit because of the high location of the amputation. However, he also knew that working to reach these goals would not give him the time to start feeling sorry for himself.

A complete leg prosthesis is built so that the hip joint rests upon a saddle and straps go around the lower torso. It works on a pendulum system, the leg propelled forward by the movement of the rest of the body. It usually takes up to three months for a patient to learn how to walk with the prosthesis. Freddie was going to learn in three weeks.

27

First of all, however, there was his appearance at the Cotton Bowl in Dallas—and Notre Dame.

On New Year's Day, 1970, the Fighting Irish broke a forty-five-year-old self-imposed ban on post-season competition by appearing in the Cotton Bowl against No. 1 Texas. Notre Dame was rated ninth in the Associated Press poll, due to an early season loss to Purdue and a tie with Southern California. The ratings, however, did not do justice to this powerful team. The Irish outweighed Texas by a good thirty pounds a man on the offensive and defensive front lines. Their defense was anchored by a 280-pound All-American giant named Mike McCoy, the offense by 175-pound All-American quarterback Joe Theisman. It would be a tough battle.

Although a press box seat had been arranged for Freddie and his family, he was determined to be with his teammates on the sidelines. And he was determined not to sit in a wheelchair. He would stand. He wanted to be treated just like any other injured football player out of uniform for the game.

His teammates were equally resolved that Freddie should still feel part of the team. The welcome was loud when he entered the Longhorn locker room before the game, but what probably pleased him most was the sight of the empty locker with the name tape that read, *Steinmark, No. 28.*

Out on the field, however, there was little to cheer about for the first three quarters of the game. Freddie stood on the sidelines, shouting and calling, supported by his crutches and Father Bomar, who kept a watchful eye on him. As the fourth quarter began, though, Notre Dame was leading, 17–14.

Then Texas began to move slowly upfield. With the clock running out, and a fourth-and-two at the Irish twelve, James Street rolled out and threw a low pass behind his best receiver, Cotton Speyrer. Speyrer pivoted back and grabbed the ball a foot off the ground at the two. Three plays later, Billy Dale bowled over for the go-ahead score.

Just as Arkansas had done less than a month before, Notre Dame fought back. And just like Arkansas, they failed, as the Texas defense intercepted a Joe Theisman pass deep in Texas territory. The Texas Longhorns were the Cotton Bowl champions, and Texas fans everywhere went crazy. The game ball went to Freddie Steinmark.

After the game, Freddie was invited by the sponsors of the Hula Bowl to fly out to Hawaii and attend their game too, but Freddie decided to decline. He would need every moment of available time to learn how to use his new leg. The big banquet was approaching—and he was going to be walking.

Although the incision was not completely healed, Freddie worked feverishly to learn how to walk again. On the night of January 12, Municipal Auditorium on the Austin campus was packed with six thousand Longhorn true-believers who had come to see the University of Texas team pick up the rewards of their season. Texas had made a clean sweep of the post-season awards—the No. 1 position in both the AP and UPI polls, plus the independently voted MacArthur and Grantland Rice trophies for finishing first. The team had easily outpolled Penn State in the final rankings.

One by one, each letterman on the team was called to the stage to accept his football letter and a ten-ounce silver medallion depicting James Street's forty-two-yard run against Arkansas. Then it was Freddie's turn. Leaning on a cane, with Scott Henderson beside him in case he should slip, Freddie rose . . . and walked to the stage.

Six thousand people, including former President and Lady Bird Johnson stood and cheered as Freddie and Scott Henderson walked across the stage to receive their rewards. The ovation seemed to go on forever. Freddie accepted his letter and medallion, smiled, then, still smiling, walked off again.

That February, living at first in a room at Father Bomar's rectory, Freddie returned to class and immediately plunged right back into his schoolwork. By now he had shifted his chemical engineering major to law and quickly raised his grades from a C average to a B.

In addition, he began accepting public speaking and television engagements, appearing on the "Today Show" with Joe Garagiola and at sportswriters' luncheons in Chicago and Philadelphia, to talk about his experiences and what had brought him through them. He learned to handle himself adeptly in front of large audiences.

"To people he did not know well, he was a quiet, gentle personality," says Father Bomar. "Later, you could see a different personality—a desire to excel personally, great ambition, concern about his own welfare.

He was constantly kidding when he wasn't worried about his own welfare.

"When his teammates got to know him, he became very popular with them. He started having a helluva good time."

His friends and former teammates found him full of life and fun. He kept whatever fears he had to himself. "After the operation we all looked up to him," says Spanky Stephens. "We couldn't have faced what he did. Yet he took it all in stride. Everyone fell in love with him. He wasn't a shy kid before and he opened himself up a lot more. Before, he was a dedicated athlete and he never drank or smoked or did much of anything. Later, when his career was over, he would go to a party and not leave at 10:30 like before, but stay until the party was over. He never got drunk, but he would enjoy a drink."

Although he began to date other girls about then, he maintained a close relationship with Linda Wheeler. Near the end of his life they made tentative plans to marry. "He might have enjoyed himself at parties, but he was a member of the old school," says Scott Henderson. "He always remained pretty true blue and loyal to Linda."

For all his schoolwork, public speaking and socializing, however, Freddie did not give up his love of sports. He worked out regularly in the weight room and began playing golf and even waterskiing. The prosthesis made it impossible for him to turn his body, but even playing on one leg, Freddie's golf score was in the mid-forties for nine holes before too long. Waterskiing, however, was a little more difficult.

"I saw him fall a million times on waterskis," says Stephens. "But when he finally got up he'd have the biggest smile on his face."

Regular trips to Houston for X-rays became part of Freddie's life. He would become tense before the checkups, but then return to his old self as soon as he was given a clean bill of health. In July, 1970, he and Father Bomar drove to J. D. Anderson Hospital for one of those regular checkups. This time the X-rays picked up several spots on his lungs. He knew this was the beginning of the end.

"If it's in my trunk, I'll be like Piccolo," he told Father Bomar on the ride back to Austin. "I'll have less than a year."

Freddie was put on chemotherapy. The long hair he had grown since his surgery started to fall out in clumps. It became important to him that no one find out about it.

That summer he was hired as an assistant coach for the Texas freshman team. To disguise the problem with his hair, he told his former teammates they should shave his head as an initiation to the coaching ranks. They did, and no one caught on. He even took the nickname "Pirate," to go with his one leg and shaved head. He enhanced the role by having his ear pierced and wearing a gold earring.

"He didn't want sympathy and pity or anything with that ring to it," says Father Bomar. "It was bitter to him and he avoided it."

His ex-teammates saw no change in him. "It was never

32

unpleasant for me or anyone else to be around him," says Henderson. "He never expressed his fears to me. He always felt something would happen and he'd be all right."

"He was wearing a toupée when I last saw him in Denver about four or five months before he died," says Red Coats, his old high school coach. "He came home to recruit some kids from the area. He'd take them out to dinner and tell them the benefits of going to Texas. He did a heck of a job."

He became busy in the Cancer Crusade as well, an activity which resulted in his receiving a special plaque from President Nixon which saluted him "for having met the challenge of cancer with the courage and spirit that marked his athletic career; for providing inspiration and hope to thousands of Americans whose lives have been touched by cancer; for his steadfast faith in God, his country and himself."

It was but one of a great many awards for courage he would receive during the last few months of his life. He always questioned whether he deserved them, however.

"I certainly don't think of myself as courageous," he wrote. "When I found out I was going to lose my leg, I cried. Is that being courageous? You don't think about being brave; my mind was filled with things I simply had to do if I was to survive. There was no choice. I think courage is doing something that you don't have to do. I was backed up to a cliff; it wasn't that I wanted to jump, I just didn't have a choice. I didn't make the decision to remove my leg. It was made for me."

Spanky Stephens dropped in to see Freddie shortly after the spots on his lungs had been found. With Freddie were several members of his family, and Stephens noticed a certain tenseness.

"I kind of figured something was wrong and he told me they had found spots on his lungs," Stephens recalls. "I told him I was really sorry. He said, 'Don't be, there was always a chance this would happen. We have to live and face the music.' He then changed the subject and talked about something funny that had happened the week before."

Freddie was admitted to the hospital on April 20, 1971. Death was thought to be imminent. It was not.

"It kinda upsets me that I go into the hospital with the flu and it makes the front pages of the paper," he told a reporter for the *Dallas Morning News*. "It really doesn't upset me, but it upsets my mother and I don't like that. But I appreciate everyone's concern. It's just that people seem to be watching me so closely."

A week before Freddie's death, Scott Henderson drove up to Houston to see him. It was the same Freddie.

"He said he was feeling better and that he was going to leave the hospital pretty soon. He was arguing with his father over little things, just like he always did. His sickness might have dented him physically, but his personality and mind were the same. I remember his voice was hoarse, probably from the chemotherapy. He asked me about what was going on back in Austin. It was small talk; I can't even remember what we talked about. It was no deathbed scene."

Near the end, Darrell Royal asked the local press to

refrain from printing stories about Freddie. The exposure was not doing him any good, the Texas coach said.

"I've just been to see him in Houston and they've had to take the television set out of his room," he told them. "That's about the only pleasure he gets these days. Every time he turns it on, though, he hears stories about Fred Steinmark's critical condition.

"Of course, he knows what he has, but he isn't giving up. He heard a report on television the other night and then told me, 'Coach, what do they mean by saying that? All I've got is a virus.' He wasn't about to concede that the cancer was whipping him."

On June 6, 1971, at about 11:00 P.M., Freddie Joe Steinmark died. He was twenty-two years old and he had been hospitalized for forty-seven days. It had been nearly eighteen months since his left leg had been amputated.

"This is one of the saddest things I've had happen to me in sports," said Fred Akers, his defensive secondary coach. "Freddie has left a huge impression on all that have been around him. We all loved him quite a lot. And he has certainly been an inspiration to countless youngsters all around the country. We will never be prouder of anyone than we are of him."

"He was a courageous young man," added Darrell Royal. "He made quite an impression on this campus and the men that follow him will feel it for years to come."

Freddie Steinmark was buried on June 9 at Mt. Olivet Cemetery in Denver, not far from Wheat Ridge High

School. Many of his coaches and teammates flew up from Austin to pay their final respects.

"I realized at the funeral what a unique family he had," says Stephens, who came up with Henderson and Mitchell. "His mom had been up all night cooking stuff. It was as if we were coming in for a reunion. Instead of you helping them, it was they who were helping you."

Football fans in Texas will find it hard to forget Freddie Steinmark. Every time the Longhorns score a touchdown, they will glance up at the Fred Steinmark Memorial Scoreboard. They will think of the smallest man on the great 1969 Texas football team, who showed at the end that he had the biggest heart.

Generations of students at Wheat Ridge High School in Denver will also remember Freddie. A bronze bust of the school's most publicized athlete sits in the office of the school's principal.

"He never wanted to become a symbol," says Scott Henderson. "He lived his life, and that was his example. He was a fine, fine young man who died at the peak of his life."

DANNY THOMPSON IS NOT REMEMBERED BY HIS FORMER teammates and coaches as an outstanding hitter or a smooth fielder. He was neither of these. What he was can best be summed up in the words of Texas Ranger General Manager Danny O'Brien shortly after Thompson's death in December, 1976.

"Danny Thompson was not the most gifted player in major league baseball," he said. "He couldn't run as fast as some, he couldn't hit with the power of most and he couldn't throw as hard as many. But he was the most complete human being I believe I've ever known. He gave the Rangers something special the past season because he always gave of himself on or off the field. To have him as a friend was a privilege. To have him as a teammate was an honor. He will be missed by our organization."

Danny Thompson was a man who always put people at ease, who refused to burden others with his problems, who never succumbed to self-pity. He was a private man with a burning desire to excel in baseball—a desire he refused to let be sidetracked by illness and nationwide publicity.

It was on February 4, 1973, that Danny Thompson found out there was something wrong with him.

Danny had enjoyed his finest season in a major league uniform in 1972. Firmly entrenched as the Minnesota Twins' starting shortstop, he had batted a solid .276, with twenty-two doubles, six triples, four home runs and forty-eight RBIs in 144 games. He had shown a knack for moving a runner along by bunting or hitting to the right side of the infield. And although he had had his share of errors, he had given the Twins a badly needed consistency at shortstop.

On that winter day in Minneapolis, however, Danny received a telephone call from Dr. Leonard Michienzi, the Twins' team physician. Four days earlier, the day before his twenty-sixth birthday, Danny had gone in for his annual team physical—weight, reflexes, blood tests, the usual routine—but this time, as Danny's father, James Thompson, remembers it, Dr. Michienzi began asking questions. Had Danny been ill lately? Had he had any colds, infections? No, Danny said, he felt terrific, everything was fine.

But it wasn't. Danny's white cell count was higher than normal, Dr. Michienzi told him, and it was imperative he have more tests immediately. Days later, Michienzi had the answer, and it hit the Thompsons like

a bombshell. Danny had leukemia. There was hope—
the type was probably acute granulocytic leukemia, the
slowest spreading strain of the disease—but it would
take still more tests to tell for sure.

Danny and Jo, his wife, traveled to the famous Mayo
Clinic in Rochester, Minnesota, and there the clinic's
Dr. Murray Silverstein examined him and in essence
repeated what Dr. Michienzi had said. But there *was*
hope—the disease could be controlled as long as it did
not become acute, he explained. "Dr. Silverstein told
Danny and Jo that he had never seen it in such an early
stage before," James Thompson says. "He told them it
might not become acute for a long time and if it did,
they might have a cure by then."

So Danny Thompson continued as he had before,
waiting and hoping—and playing baseball.

Danny Thompson was born on February 1, 1947, in
Wichita, Kansas. Shortly thereafter, his family moved
across the Kansas border to the town of Capron in north-
west Oklahoma, a small wheat-growing hamlet with a
population of sixty-two.

Danny's love for sports came from his father, who
had been a track and football star on an Elkhart,
Kansas, high school team that had included Glenn Cun-
ningham, the famed Olympic miler. After high school,
where he had won fourteen letters, the elder Thompson
had been offered a contract with a professional baseball
team in Wichita, but because he lacked the transporta-
tion, he was forced to give up his chance. For this reason,
he wanted his sons to have every opportunity possible.

"We put baseball first," he says, and always saw to it that his boys—older brother Jimmy and younger brother Monty included—played plenty of baseball. "Danny started playing Little League ball when he was nine years old, back in the third grade. We used to drive him out to Alva," a town twelve miles away. Every week without fail, the Thompsons would pack the boys and two girls—Sheila and Phoebe, both still in diapers—into the back seat of the family car and make that drive. Chores around the house always were secondary.

It was soon evident that Danny was the one most interested in making baseball his career. Monty had the talent, his father says, but lost some of his competitive edge while on a baseball scholarship at Oklahoma State. Danny, however, was single-minded.

"Ever since he was a little kid, that was all he wanted to do," says his father. "Every time he went out on the baseball field, he played his heart out."

For all the emphasis on baseball, though, Danny and the others did help out with the family business: Thompsons' Sundries, a combination restaurant, grocery and hardware store they not only owned but lived in. They helped out, too, with the sheep, pigs, chickens and rabbits stocked on the three-hundred-foot lot. Danny, like all the younger Thompsons, belonged to the Future Farmers of America. "Danny came up with several champion sheep," remembers James. "I think one year he won a first prize for the entire state of Oklahoma."

On Sundays, the Thompson clan were regulars at the local Methodist church in Capron. His father has a hard time remembering any problems with Danny. "I wouldn't say he was perfect, though," he notes. "I did catch him smoking once. He was about seven or eight at the time."

Then, in 1954, James Thompson became seriously ill with a rare blood disease called Pickwick's Syndrome. The disease caused him to retain tremendous amounts of water and bloat up to 425 pounds. He would tire with the least amount of physical activity. Although the business had done well, Danny's mother was forced to sell the store while his father lay near death in the Little Rock, Arkansas, Veterans' Hospital, and move the family to Waldron, Kansas, to open a grocery store there. Later, after James recovered, the family returned to Capron.

The Thompsons remained split for several years more, however, when James obtained a job as a nurse's aide at a Wichita veterans' hospital. He worked there during the week and was forced to commute to Capron on weekends. Years later, he obtained a job closer to home as a petroleum salesman.

Danny started playing professional baseball when he was fifteen for an American Legion team in Enid, Oklahoma. By this time, he was well on his way to a solid six feet, 185 pounds. He was also playing for the local high school team in Capron, first as a catcher and then as a pitcher, amassing a record of 37–7 as a pitcher. In one eleven-inning game, he fanned thirty-three batters, and lost only when the catcher was charged with a passed ball.

His record was all the more remarkable since at Capron High School there were only thirteen boys— and all of them were on the baseball team. Danny's high school graduating class consisted of a grand total of four students, which led to a standing joke several years later

43

with the Twins. "He used to say he graduated third in his class," says Dave Goltz, who broke into the Twins organization with Danny in 1968. "Yet, he had trouble getting into college—because he wasn't in the top half."

In fact, Danny had little trouble getting into college. The real decision for him was whether he wanted to go at all.

Immediately after his high school graduation, Danny was drafted by the New York Yankees in June, 1965—the chance of a lifetime, he thought. He was anxious to begin his baseball career, but his parents convinced him that the opportunity would still be there in a few years.

"The Yankees only offered $8,000," says James Thompson, "and Danny decided it was best to take the full scholarship at OSU. It was his decision, though. I never pushed my kids to do anything."

Although his high school sweetheart and future wife enrolled at Oklahoma University, Danny was swayed by Chet Bryan, the Oklahoma State baseball coach, to enroll at the Stillwater, Oklahoma, campus. Bryan, who coached the team for thirteen years until his retirement in 1977, says simply, "He came to State because he had been following their games on the radio since he was a boy."

After getting some extra polish during the summers as a member of the Rapid City entry in the Basin League, a college league composed of some of the best young talent in the country, Danny arrived at Oklahoma State and quickly began to shine.

"He was the best kid I've ever worked with," says Bryan, who coached Danny in 1967 and 1968. "He was just a little special and he played that way. He was dedicated and that's the type of boy a coach enjoys working with. He was a winner."

Bryan, who still lives in the Stillwater area and now handles the equipment for the State football team, remembers Danny as a religious young man, who made up in desire what he lacked in superlative talent.

"I questioned his chances of making the big leagues on account of his speed," says Bryan. "I didn't think he would ever play shortstop in the majors. He was not an outstanding player. I've had kids who could outthrow him, outrun him, out everything him. Yet, he made himself by determination."

Oklahoma State enjoyed two fine years during Danny's stay with them. In 1967, they finished seventh in the national baseball tourney. The next year, they won the Big Eight tourney and went on to finish fifth in the nationals behind the all-around play of All-American shortstop Danny Thompson.

Before that season, however, Danny had had to make a decision: the Washington Senators wanted him to leave school and play for them. "He was drafted by Washington and offered $10,000 to sign," recalls Bryan. "He could have left then, but he felt he owed the university another year because we had given him a scholarship. The Washington scout stayed mad at me for a long time, even though it was all Danny's decision."

Danny remained in school through his junior year and the gamble paid off. In June, he was drafted again, by the Minnesota Twins, and this time he signed. With his bride of several months, he packed his bags and

45

drove north to his first major baseball assignment: St. Cloud (Minnesota) of the Rookie League.

He showed potential immediately, batting .282 and fielding well at shortstop in his year with St. Cloud. That winter, he played in the Instructional League in St. Petersburg, Florida, with Dave Goltz.

"You felt like you knew him right away and could talk to him about anything," says Goltz, the tall, blond left-hander, who became a Twin in 1972. "He was very close to his parents, who were the same type he was. They were all very nice, easy to know. You felt like you knew all of them for years after just talking to them for five or ten minutes."

That winter in the Instructional League, Goltz and Thompson and Jerry Terrell, later an infielder with the Twins and Kansas City Royals, shared a trailer home. It soon became apparent to his two roommates what Danny's biggest talent was.

"He could outeat anyone," says Goltz. "He loved to eat steaks and large meals and he had a very fast metabolism, so he never gained any weight. When we roomed together, we would cook steaks and then eat sandwiches while waiting for the steaks to cook. I'd put on weight, but Danny never did."

The following spring, Danny was promoted to the Twins' Double-A affiliate, Charleston, in the Southern League. He was performing extremely well with the club and had been named to the league all-star team over such competition as Dave Concepcion of the Asheville club, later a star with the Cincinnati Reds. With his .302 batting average, many considered Danny the finest shortstop in Double-A ball. Then his career nearly came to an abrupt end in July, 1969.

Danny was chasing a routine fly ball during a game with Columbus (Georgia) when he smashed violently into an outfielder who was running in at full speed. The sickening sound of the two bodies colliding could be heard throughout the ballpark. Danny was gingerly removed from the outfield grass by stretcher and taken by ambulance to a local hospital, where it was found he had a broken nose and jaw, a smashed cheekbone and a fractured ankle.

"Terrell and myself were in the Army at Fort Rucker, Alabama, when we heard about Danny's accident," says Goltz. "We rented a car and put 475 miles on it to visit Danny at the hospital. When we got there, there was no one to tell us where to go, so we walked from room to room looking for him. If his wife had not been sitting on the bed, we never would have recognized him."

Danny was a mess. He had to undergo plastic surgery and was hospitalized for weeks. Even after he was patched up, he continued to have problems with his sinuses. No one was sure if he could come back—but they needn't have worried. He made a fast recovery. That winter he played ball for Arecibo in the Puerto Rican League and made the all-star team, batting .267.

In 1970 Danny spent spring training with the Twins in Orlando, Florida, and impressed both manager Bill Rigney and owner Calvin Griffith by batting .320 in eleven games. Since the Twins were still set at shortstop, however, with Leo Cardenas, they decided to farm him out for one more year at Evansville, their Triple-A team.

Danny started slowly with the Indiana team, but his average was up to .247 by the end of June, with twelve doubles, four triples and five stolen bases. He and third baseman Eric Soderholm, later a member of the Twins and Chicago White Sox, were settling in as the parent club's main hopes for the future.

Then, on June 22, the future arrived. Twin second baseman Rod Carew was pivoting to make a double play against the Milwaukee Brewers when base runner Mike Hegan barreled into him with a hard slide. Carew limped off the field; an examination revealed torn ligaments and detached knee cartilage in his right knee. Carew—the leading hitter in the league in 1969 and batting .366 at the time—would have to undergo immediate surgery. He would be through for most of the season, if not all of it. The call went down to Evansville.

James Thompson remembers that day well. Danny and his Evansville team were in Wichita to play a road game and the elder Thompson was just getting ready to go to the ballpark to see his son play.

"I was working at the Wichita VA hospital and staying in nurse's quarters at the time," remembers Thompson. "Just as I was going out on the back porch, my phone started ringing. I nearly broke my neck getting to the phone. I picked up the phone and it was Danny.

"He said, 'Daddy, if you're gonna come watch the ballgame, I'm not gonna be there.' I said, 'You hurt, son?' He said, 'No, I'm a big leaguer now. I'm gonna catch the first plane out of here.' "

Danny flew out of Wichita to Minneapolis that night, to replace the best hitter in baseball. It was not the easiest way to break in. Not only was he moving into a new position, but into the starting lineup of a veteran team that was used to winning.

While Carew was an important ingredient in the club's success formula, the Twins were loaded with talent. The big bats on the 1970 Twins belonged to such sluggers as Harmon Killebrew, Bob Allison, Tony Oliva and Cesar Tovar. The pitching was in the very capable arms of Jim Perry, Luis Tiant, Jim Kaat, Tom Hall and a nineteen-year-old whiz kid from Holland named Bert Blyleven. Thompson and Blyleven were to room together for several years.

The manager was Bill Rigney, who had replaced the winning, but always troublesome, Billy Martin during the off-season. It was the first, but hardly the last, time Martin would be relieved of his managerial duties. Although Minnesota had won the Western Division of the American League in 1969 before dropping three straight in the playoffs in Baltimore, the fiery Martin had punched two Minnesota team executives and one Twin pitcher, and everyone had known he wouldn't be long for Minnesota.

The day of Danny's arrival in Milwaukee, the Twins were in front by four games in the West. The Minneapolis newspapers expressed doubt, however, over whether the Twins would be able to maintain their lead over the two good young clubs in the league—the Oakland A's and California Angels—with an untried, inexperienced second baseman.

Danny made his debut in a 4–1 loss to the Brewers. He went hitless in four trips to the plate, but handled every chance in the field flawlessly. The next day was the same, but then, in a game against Chicago, Danny broke out with a vengeance, singling twice and driving in a run in the Twins' 9–1 triumph.

During that rookie year, Danny became close to the Twins' team leader, Harmon Killebrew. One of the American League's first "bonus babies," the Idaho man said little, but let his bat speak for him. Built like a moose, with short, thick forearms and a torso like a fullback, "Killer" was usually good for thirty-five to forty home runs a year and a hundred-plus runs batted in.

"Danny was a very hard worker," says Killebrew, who later went to the Royals before returning to Minnesota as the club's television announcer. "In fact, he worked too hard. He would take as many as a thousand ground balls before a game. He was pretty quiet and never really said that much. He was a fine young man though, the kind you'd like your son to be."

By the beginning of August, the Twins had a ten-game lead over California and looked like a sure thing to ease into their second divisional title and a rematch in the playoffs with Baltimore. Then suddenly, the team's play began to disintegrate. The double plays were not being turned over, the hits failed to drop in, the pitching fell apart. The Twins lost nine straight games and soon found themselves only four and a half games in front of Oakland and five ahead of California.

Danny, however, had filled in well for Carew at second base. He was fielding sharply and, as late as August 25, was hitting .282, including a modest seven-game hitting streak at the beginning of August.

Still, the lead dwindled to three over California and five and a half over Oakland after the Twins were bombed by Cleveland, 14–1, on August 29. Danny seemed to be pressing at the plate, and Rigney replaced him for several games with Frank Quilici, a utility infielder who would later manage the club.

The Twins flew west in September for two three-game series—first with the Angels, then with the A's—that would likely decide the title.

The team approached both series with trepidation, but they needn't have worried. Blyleven blanked the Angels, 4–0; the Twins won the second game when Danny smacked a single through the infield to score Tovar for what proved to be the winning run; and the most the Angels could muster the next day was one run against the Twins' three. Oakland got the same treatment. The Twins swept the A's 3–1, 6–1 and 7–2, and for all practical purposes secured their second consecutive Western Division crown.

Danny, however, had begun to feel as if he were hitting in quicksand. One coach said, "He looked as if he was going to squeeze the bat in two, he was trying so hard."

A knowledgeable hitter even then, Danny knew there was something seriously wrong with his stance. It was easier for him to discover the problem, however, than to correct the flaw.

"I'm doing a lot of things at the plate I wasn't doing before," he told a newsman with some disgust. "For one thing, I'm collapsing my leg which I did earlier in the season. I finally edged out of it. Now I'm back doing it.

When I do this I drop the back part of my body and I am behind the ball. I can't get the ball out in front. The result is that I pop everything up. I can't hit anything on the ground. I must have hit fifteen fly balls to first, second and right field in the last few games."

Nevertheless, Danny was given the starting nod in the playoff series against the Baltimore Orioles, and he jumped into it with his usual enthusiasm. Unfortunately, it was to be a short series.

The Orioles had finished the 1970 season with a 108–54 record, the best in baseball, led by the pitching of Jim Palmer, Dave McNally and Mike Cuellar and the power of Frank and Brooks Robinson. They proceeded to crush the Twins in only three days, exactly as they had in 1969. After scores of 10–6, 11–3 and 6–1, they went on to meet the Reds in the World Series—and clobber them too, in five games. The season was suddenly over.

Although Danny finished the year with a low .219 batting average and had made few people associated with the Twins forget Rod Carew, the consensus was that he had gotten the job done.

After a winter of playing golf, he came to spring training wondering what his role would be with the 1971 Twins. Carew was healthy again and Cardenas was a fixture at shortstop. It did not take long for Danny to see that this would not be his year.

On a cold, damp April day at Yankee Stadium, Danny was at third base as a defensive replacement when, fielding a ground ball, his back foot slipped and he felt pain in his arm as he threw the runner out at first. The next day he woke up with a sore arm, a lump under his arm-pit and a discolored rib cage. Although the team doctors gave him every imaginable test, they never found out what was wrong with him. His father, however, believes this is when the leukemia may first have appeared. "The doctors are still not really sure why he got injured," he says.

After that, Danny went to the ballpark every day to receive heat treatments and a massage, but played very few games (only forty-eight) and batted .263 in fifty-seven appearances at the plate.

He did, however, acquire one thing during this painful season—a nickname. When Danny first arrived from Evansville, he had a powerful throwing arm and was called "Shotgun." Now, with his arm shooting blanks, Killebrew gave him the name "Chicken Wing." This eventually was shortened to "Chicky."

It was also a rough year for the Minnesota team. The Twins finished in fifth place behind Oakland, Kansas City, Chicago and California, twenty-four games off their 1970 pace. Nevertheless, there was encouraging news for Danny.

In November, the Twins traded Cardenas and named Danny the heir apparent to the shortstop job. Although the doctors told him to rest his "chicken wing" during the off-season, he immediately began a strengthening program, and after months of torturous exercises, lifting weights and throwing for hours at a basement wall, he managed to build his right arm back.

It paid off: 1972 was an excellent year for Danny—but the rest of the Twins slumped. Killebrew's home-run production fell to twenty-six and he batted just .231. Not one starting pitcher had a winning record, and the best Blyleven could manage was 17–17. Owner Griffith became disenchanted with Bill Rigney and replaced him with Frank Quilici midway through the season. The club finished behind Oakland and Chicago.

Then that winter, just as he was beginning to gear himself up mentally for the coming spring training, Danny got the news of his leukemia. He was puzzled— after all, he felt fine—and resolved to keep the news of his white cell count to himself. He did not want anyone —management, teammates or fans—feeling sorry for him. But the news got out anyway.

"The day after he found out, we had the second annual Danny Thompson Pool Tournament in his basement," remembers Tom Mee, the Twins' public relations director. "Some of the guys from the club were there and lots of beer and potato chips and pretzels. We all had a good time. He never said a word about it."

About two weeks later, a brief note by a sports columnist on the *Minneapolis Tribune* made Danny's condition public. Soon he was known everywhere as "the baseball player with leukemia."

While his teammates accepted him with or without the illness, it was different for the press. In every city he visited during the exhibition season, there would be new reporters assigned to write the same old story. Letters started pouring in from all over the country. The letter writers were people with leukemia or those whose friends or relatives suffered from the disease.

Playing regularly during the beginning of the 1973

season kept Danny's mind relatively free, and his play seemed to be totally unaffected. Then, however, he started suffering from minor leg pulls and other assorted muscle aches. As he later told Al Sperber, a radio broadcaster in New York City, he started wondering if the leukemia was causing the injuries—but Dr. Silverstein reassured him. "Play ball," the doctor said. "You're no more or less prone to muscle aches than anyone."

That was easier said than done. Danny couldn't forget about it, and the Twins' management wasn't helping any.

"I think a lot of people then were waiting for me to go downhill when they knew what I had," Danny told a reporter a year later. "But it was just a lot of injuries, one after the other. My attitude was bad. I wasn't playing and when I was, I got hurt.

"By the end of the year it got so bad I didn't want to go to the park. I can say my condition wasn't a big reason for me getting so down, but in the back of my mind it might have been."

It was tough for Danny to adjust to his condition that first year. While most of his teammates never realized what was going on inside his mind, sudden doubts and insecurities continued to plague him. Road trips were toughest, according to his father. He began wondering when the leukemia was going to start affecting him and what would happen to his family if he died.

It was only his wife, Jo, that kept him from feeling too sorry for himself that year, Danny told Sperber. Although Danny had a miserable season, batting .225 in 99 games and playing poorly in the field, Jo refused to accept the illness as an excuse for his poor play. She would goad him into trying to forget about the leukemia, and start thinking about playing ball.

Danny's own inner resources had a good deal to do with it too, however. "He finally just looked at it as this is the way it was meant to be," says his father. Bert Blyleven, who was a close friend of Danny's for most of their years together in Minnesota, concurs. "When Danny found out he had leukemia in 1973, he went through some hard times personally for a while, which has to be a normal reaction," Blyleven told a reporter. "He dreaded it, he resented it, he really fought it. His personality went through some changes.

"But it didn't surprise any of us that Danny got it all back together after a while. Danny was a special person to begin with and he wasn't going to let this destroy that. After he was able to accept his condition and live with it, I thought he became even more of a beautiful person than before."

The change in Danny was subtle. He was not the type to burden others with his problems and doubts. Most of his teammates said they never saw any change in him.

"As far as I could tell he didn't change at all after his illness was disclosed," says Killebrew. "I know he didn't want any sympathy. He didn't want people to say look at poor Danny Thompson out there at shortstop who just made an error because he's ill."

During his lowest period, Danny found something to help him hurdle the mental obstacle—religion.

Raised in the Methodist Church in Capron, Danny had always been fairly religious. He had even been awarded a five-year pin for never missing Sunday School, his father remembers, and served as president of the Methodist Youth Fellowship in his hometown. It was not until he became aware of his illness, however, that he became truly devout.

Jim Kaat, a pitcher with the Twins that year, drew Danny out of his shell and convinced him to join the team's weekly chapel services and start reading the Bible. He began to attend meetings where members of the Fellowship of Christian Athletes would speak.

"I remember the thing he did most was read the Bible," says Larry Hisle, Danny's roommate for two seasons with the Twins. "I know he even talked a few fellas on the team into reading it themselves."

Danny felt more at peace with himself after his religious awakening. Often he would spend the night after a game in his hotel room with one or another of his teammates, huddled over the Bible. He found he was no longer scared of the shadow that hovered over him. While he was still determined to beat the leukemia, he no longer was afraid of the thought that he might die from it.

In October, 1973, Danny went to the Mayo Clinic for a checkup and was told his white cell count had jumped to more than two hundred thousand from a count of twenty-five thousand in February. The normal white cell figure is between five and ten thousand. Dr. Silverstein had prescribed no treatment up to now, but "now is the time," he said, "to begin chemotherapy."

Danny began taking the drug myleran to lower his white cell count, and also started another "medication" under strict orders from his doctor: several bottles of beer a day. Beer, the doctor told Danny, would flush out his system and, like the myleran, lower his white cell count.

When the chemotherapy was far enough advanced, the immunization program began. Live leukemia cells were injected into his body in the hopes that Danny's immunization system would be awakened by the foreign substance and begin destroying both the new and the old diseased white blood cells. It was an experimental technique and Danny was one of the first it had been tried on at the clinic. The first year Danny was given six shots, the second year four and gradually the injections became fewer as the need became less.

"He would get violently sick from the injections," remembers Dave Goltz. "At the end, he would be sick for as long as three days. It was like the flu, and it would really knock him out."

In addition, the injections left raw, crusty blotches on his arm that his oldest daughter, Tracy, called pepperonis. A boil would form after the shot, which would eventually open, releasing streams of pus. Danny never complained, except about the dozens of T-shirts he stained. The injections seemed to be helping, though.

Nevertheless, the Twins had written Danny off by the time he appeared for spring training in 1974. Arriving in Orlando, he found five other shortstops competing for his job, and, after hitting less than .200 during the exhibition season, Danny became the third-string shortstop behind Sergio Ferrer and Jerry Terrell. Injuries at other positions and Ferrer's eight errors in eleven games, however, moved Danny back into the starting lineup.

Although the 1974 Twins were again a third-place club, the team finished strongly. Danny batted .250 in ninety-seven games, played well at shortstop and, for the most part, put the leukemia out of his head.

"I really wouldn't know I had it if the doctors didn't tell me I did," Danny told a New York City sportswriter. "My doctor tells me I'm in as good shape as half the guys on the team. At the Mayo Clinic, they said playing ball was the best thing for me. There's no use crying or sitting around. I've got a lot of spunk in me and I'm gonna use it up.

"I've gotten a lot of letters from people with the same thing who say what I've got gives them hope. If I can help some people. . . . They're gonna find a cure for this thing, they're close to a breakthrough, every day they're finding new stuff."

The 1974 season was not pain-free for Danny, however. In April, a thigh muscle pull put him on the disabled list for thirty days, and though he was ready to be removed from the list in May, Griffith and Quilici at first were not ready to take him back—Quilici told Danny there was a roster problem and to be patient. Griffith said it was less complicated than that. Quilici had told him that Danny was no longer a major league shortstop. In addition, the team physician had told both of them that Danny's leukemia was worsening.

A quick call to Dr. Silverstein at the Mayo Clinic found this not to be the case. Eventually Danny returned to the lineup.

Later in the year, Bobby Murcer gave him a spike wound that went down to the bone, and though the injury was serious, this time Danny was not taking any chances with the management. He went back to work the next day.

Meanwhile, Griffith was aggravating the situation by telling the Minnesota newspapers, "What the Twins need to become a championship caliber team is a shortstop." Danny's teammates thought a lot more of him.

"He was a good man for the ballclub," says Tony Oliva, a superb hitter with the Twins who was forced to become a coach because of damaged legs. "Danny was always working hard to improve himself. He tried to help the ballclub any way he could. Even though he was sick, it was hard for me to believe it. He never let you think about it. He was a good shortstop and a pretty good hitter. He worked very hard to be a good hitter. After he got sick he kept working harder. He was able to play, but the manager [Quilici] thought he was sick. Danny felt God had a plan for everyone, and if this was the way He wanted it, there was nothing he could do."

"He was not an All-Star shortstop, not even a regular all the time," Harmon Killebrew adds. "But he was the most courageous young man, to see the shots and the reaction to the shots."

During the 1974 season, Danny was happy to see that the fans also were beginning to forget about his leukemia. During one game, he made two errors in one inning, to a chorus of loud boos. "That was super," Danny later said. "I didn't want people saying, 'Oh, he's

60

got leukemia, he can make erorrs.' They booed the hell out of me and I loved it. I knew they were accepting me as a ballplayer."

In August, Danny and Larry Hisle became roommates. The tendency with most clubs is to room blacks with blacks and whites with whites, but this time a late season deal had left an uneven number of black players. Quilici asked Danny if he would be interested in rooming on the road with Hisle.

Danny was delighted. Hisle, who had played part-time with the Philadelphia Phillies before being dealt to the Twins in 1973, was on his way to becoming a star in Minnesota. Four years later, he would receive $3 million as a free agent from the Milwaukee Brewers in a spirited bidding war, but in 1974, he was just a well-respected, very popular player with the team.

The two of them, in fact, had become close during Hisle's first year in Minnesota, brought together by their mutual love for sports, particularly college football. A native of Portsmouth, Ohio, Larry was a big fan of the Ohio State University football team, and Danny of the University of Oklahoma's, and the two men were always making one-dollar bets. "When he moved in with Larry," Dave Goltz notes, "it wasn't a question of black and white, but how Oklahoma and Ohio State would get along."

"I guess Danny was the type of person everybody would like to be," Larry Hisle says now. "He taught me a lot about people. Where there was a time to be serious, he was serious, yet he had the ability to laugh and enjoy

61

himself. He could even laugh at himself. But basically, he was just a real genuine person, a person you enjoyed being around."

One evidence of Danny's sense of humor was a joke he played on Dave Goltz.

"There were rumors that winter that I was going to be traded to Texas or Detroit," Goltz recalls. "I don't know how Danny even knew about it because he was back home in Burlington [Oklahoma]. Anyway, I got a phone call from someone who said he was with Texas. Your heart kind of stops when you hear something like that and I didn't say anything for a while. Then all of a sudden I heard the guy on the phone laugh and I knew it was Danny."

Shortly thereafter, in February, 1975, Danny received the Hutch Award, named after Fred Hutchinson, a former pitcher with the Detroit Tigers and manager of the St. Louis Cardinals and Cincinnati Reds. Hutchinson died of cancer in 1964, and the annual award is given to the player "who best exemplifies his courageous spirit." Danny was proud of that, but for the most part, 1975 was not a banner year for him. Although Griffith had told Danny the job was his during spring training, that wasn't the case as he found himself alternating with Sergio Ferrer and Luis Gomez, a former basketball player at UCLA.

As he later admitted, Danny pouted through much of the early part of the 1975 season. He was unnerved when a coach told him he would have been released during the spring if Quilici had not fought to keep him.

By the end of the year, however, Danny was playing

regularly again, and ended up batting a solid .270 with five home runs, his highest total in the majors. His fielding had left something to be desired, though; he made twenty-six errors in 112 games, hardly the stuff Golden Gloves are made of. The Twins played well during the final months of the season, but finished in their customary also-ran position, third, with a 76–83 record. After the last game, Quilici and his coaching crew were fired, and Danny went to speak to Griffith before heading back to Oklahoma.

Player and owner talked briefly about the season, and Griffith gave no indication Danny would be playing any more regularly in 1976 than he had in 1975. He even suggested that Danny look further into a suggested coaching job at Oklahoma State. Obviously, Danny knew, this was not something you discussed with a player for whom you had plans.

Oklahoma coach Chet Bryan had been talking with Danny for several years about coaching at his alma mater. "I kept telling him to go back to school and get his degree because I intended to push him for my job. I was hoping he'd play two or three more years and then come here."

That winter Danny and Jo, and the two girls, Tracy, six, and Dana, two, set up housekeeping in the large, comfortable, old farmhouse in Burlington they had purchased the year before from Jo's parents. He rented most of the land that came with it out to farmers in the area, but he kept some of it for his cattle, horses and dogs.

Danny also decided to go back to school for the first time since 1968, and enrolled as a first semester senior at Northwestern Oklahoma State College in Alva. As he worked his way through fifteen credit hours in his major —health, physical education and recreation—he made plans to complete his degree in a couple of years. His mind was always on the future.

The future gave him a jolt, however, when he received his contract for the 1976 season in the mail. Danny was making $27,500 a year, an extremely low figure for a major leaguer going into his seventh season, and had wanted a $3,500 raise. Instead, Griffith offered him a $500 cut in salary. Danny threatened to play out his option.

Griffith, who was not known for his profligacy around salary time, finally came up with a $2,000 raise. Danny, however, decided he had had enough and talked about becoming a free agent.

"I figured an expansion team would take me for sure in 1977," Danny told a reporter. "But when I told Calvin that, he said, 'Nobody wants you. Who's going to sign a ballplayer who's going to break down overnight?' I don't think he meant it that way, but that's the way it came out. He didn't have to say that to sign me to a contract."

Whether he meant it or not, that was in fact the way Griffith had looked at Danny since that winter day back in 1973. "The Twins put a stop on me when they found out about my disease," Danny said. "They said I couldn't do this, couldn't do that. It was a sad situation."

Under new manager Gene Mauch, Danny played part-time for the Twins in 1976, batting .234 in thirty-four games. Then, on June 1, he got the news. He had been traded to the Texas Rangers.

"He was happy to be going," remembers Tony Oliva. "He would be close to home and would have a chance to play a little more."

Danny was a throw-in in a trade that sent Bert Blyleven to Texas for young infielders Roy Smalley and Mike Cubbage and pitchers Bill Singer and Jim Gideon.

"I'm shocked but happy," Danny told a Dallas reporter. "All I'd heard the past few days had been about Bert going to Texas. My name was never mentioned until today.

"I got a call from a guy saying he was Danny O'Brien, general manager of the Texas Rangers, and he said that Texas wanted me in the Blyleven deal. I thought it was Dave Goltz playing a trick on me [and paying him back] so I said 'quit kidding.' Finally I got it through my head that it was O'Brien and I was going to Texas."

O'Brien asked Danny how much he had been making in Minnesota and how much he had asked for. Then he said he'd top it with an offer for $38,000 if Danny signed with the Rangers immediately.

"It took me one second to make up my mind," Danny said. "In three minutes I was making a salary I had only dreamed about in six years with the Twins."

Danny understood that, with the skills of Toby Harrah at shortstop and Lenny Randle at second base, manager Frank Lucchesi would most likely use him in spot situations only, at least at first. That was all right with him. He knew he would get his chance.

That chance came in his first start against the White Sox on June 4, when Randle was forced to sit out with a muscle pull. Nearly 25,000 fans filled Arlington Stadium that day, twice as many as the Twins ordinarily pulled on a good day in Metropolitan Stadium.

Danny singled his first trip to the plate in the first inning, slammed a three-run homer in the second, then an RBI-scoring double in the fourth and finally a ground single in the fifth to cap a perfect day in the Rangers' 14–3 rout. When he stepped up for his final time at bat, he received a standing ovation.

"I didn't know what to do," he said after the game. "I'd never had a standing ovation before. I had goose bumps all over. I didn't know whether to stand there or get in and hit or what."

Blyleven, who knew Danny well, understood how he felt.

"We were talking about it the next day and he said it was the first time his mind had ever gone blank in the middle of a game," Blyleven later told a reporter. "He said he wanted to step out of the batter's box and tip his hat or something, but that he didn't want to look like a hot dog. So he just stood there in a daze. Danny said the pitcher could have gone ahead and made the pitch and he'd never have known it."

In the clubhouse after the game, his new teammates joked about Danny's role in the big trade. "Hey," cracked catcher Jim Sundberg, "who's the other guy in the Danny Thompson trade?"

By this time, Danny had become more comfortable letting people know of his ailment. He began visiting children with cancer in hospitals throughout the country.

"I don't know if it's good for me; I really get depressed," he said. "But I guess it's good for the kids. I remember one kid in Detroit who had a few days to live. A year later, though, I was at the ballpark when a man took me over to meet his son. It was the same kid. And he had a cast on his leg. He had broken it sliding into second base in a ballgame. I felt so good I had chills all over.

"I guess I do give a lot of people a lot of hope by playing. If it makes other people feel good, then it makes me feel good. And they're going to come up with a cure soon."

Danny finished the year in Texas with a .214 average for sixty-four games. The figures weren't remarkable, but he impressed his teammates with the way he gave himself up to move runners up a base.

"The thing about Danny is that he gives me peace of mind when he's playing," said Frank Lucchesi, who told reporters that the only time he was ever aware of Danny's illness was when he asked permission to leave to get his shots. "He'd usually find a way to help the ballclub."

Toby Harrah agreed. "In just the short time he was with the Rangers, he left such a positive effect," said Harrah. "He was always doing something to pull us up every game."

Dave Goltz, who kept in touch with Danny by telephone, felt the four months in Texas had been good for him.

"He was tired of being played as a sick person; he

just wanted to be a ballplayer," Goltz says. "He was much more relaxed in Texas."

Goltz and Danny had planned to travel to Silver Creek, Nebraska, on November 3, 1976, for the Grand National Mixed Bag Hunt. The event would pit hunters from the Twins against those from the Royals. Goltz and Danny had often gone hunting together in Minnesota for grouse or deer.

"He called around that time to say the doctors told him he shouldn't be going out in crowds," Goltz says. "I could tell there was something wrong by the tone of his voice. Danny loved to hunt. He just didn't want anyone to feel sorry for him, but I could tell something wasn't right. Apparently he knew then."

Apparently he did. His spleen had become swollen and his white cell count uncontrollable. He entered the Mayo Clinic on November 16. His spleen was removed on December 3.

"It was hushed up, but I found out about it and I called his wife and told her I would come down," recalls Killebrew, who now lives in Oregon. "She said, 'Danny wouldn't want you to come down.' He still had hopes of making the Texas ballclub in 1977 and he didn't want anyone to know he was sick.

"Later, I called him in the hospital. He was still fighting to the very end. His spleen, which they had just removed, weighed ten pounds, while a normal spleen weighs about a pound. Did he talk of his future? He wanted to continue playing in the big leagues for another four or five years."

At 6:07 P.M. on December 10, 1976, Danny Thompson died from complications caused by the leukemia, nearly four years after it had been discovered in his body. He was two months short of his thirtieth birthday.

More than five hundred friends and relatives paid their respects to Danny at a memorial service held at the Burlington High School gymnasium.

On a cool, sunny day, he was buried in a flat, treeless cemetery in his native town of Capron. Less than twenty yards away, cattle grazed quietly on stalks of green wheat.

Harmon Killebrew did not forget about his good friend, Danny Thompson. He was not content with the memories. Along with his partner, Ralph Harding, a former Idaho congressman, he set up the annual Danny Thompson Memorial Golf Tournament in Sun Valley, Idaho, shortly after Danny's death. The event now draws some of the biggest names in politics and sports, including former President Gerald Ford, Speaker of the House Tip O'Neill, Mickey Mantle and Stan Musial. The proceeds from the tournament go to the University of Minnesota Leukemia Research Fund. In 1978, with more than 200 golfers participating, the tournament raised $42,000.

"Desire was the thing that was most typical of him," Harmon Killebrew says of Danny Thompson. "He was a man who loved the game, who loved to play ball."

JOE ROTH

JOE ROTH WAS SPECIAL TO THE PEOPLE WHO KNEW HIM, not just to those who knew of him.

He was an All-American who could pass a football with as much ease as it takes most people to walk. Yet his ability in football was incidental. His existence as a man was much more than that.

"It's amazing to me that he has broken the hearts of students on one of the most cynical campuses in the country," said Father Michael Hunt during a memorial mass for Joe at Newman Hall on the University of California at Berkeley campus.

"Whether they were churchgoers or not," Father Hunt later said, "they knew inside that this guy really had it —that he represented the best of what the human spirit could be. He stood for goodness and decency—not in a stupid or sentimental way, but in a profound way."

This feeling was echoed by the man who was his coach during the 1975 and 1976 football seasons at Berkeley. Mike White had a ringside seat for the show of courage and determination Joe put on during his final football season.

"On and off the field, Joe was the finest individual I have ever been associated with in athletics," White says. "Joe had an impact on everyone he came in contact with."

"You hear about this guy and you want to say 'Is he for real?' " adds his quarterback coach, Paul Hackett. "He was so special that it's very difficult for others to comprehend."

Joe Roth was born and raised in San Diego, the youngest son of a production engineer who had never finished high school. The middle brother, Tom, was eleven years older; the eldest brother, John, fourteen years older. Tom Roth had been a starting quarterback for the Washington State Cougars in the mid-1960s when Joe was just beginning to learn the rudiments of the game, and Joe was always in a headlong rush to catch up to him.

"He was never a little kid," Lawrence Roth once said of Joe. "With Tom being eleven years older, he had to act like one of the big boys from the start." One of the things the "big boys" did was play football.

Joe's football career began when he entered his local high school, Granite Hills, in 1969, though he hardly took the school by storm. He spent his first year as the freshman quarterback and his second as the starting signal caller for the junior varsity. It wasn't until his junior year that he made varsity.

A tall, gangly, awkward-looking kid—while he stood nearly six feet four inches, he barely weighed 165 pounds—Joe got the job done even if he didn't look especially fluid doing it.

"He was always very dedicated and intelligent in his knowledge of the game," says Jim Symington, his coach at Granite Hills and later an assistant coach at Joe's next school, Grossmont Junior College. "He was an extremely coachable kid, a coach's dream. He always knew what you were trying to convey to him. . . . He was very mature. His parents were older than most parents, but they were very supportive and involved. It seemed like he never went through the stages most young kids go through."

Joe improved from game to game during his high school career, ending his senior season in a burst of glory when the good, but hardly overpowering, Granite Hills team won its last five games.

Coach Symington remembers two of those games in particular: the one against Grossmont High School, for instance—a powerhouse that had beaten Granite Hills nine times out of ten. With Joe at the helm, the underdogs moved the ball up the field at will and upset Grossmont, 14–0, "with the score not indicative of the game," Symington says.

There was also the game against El Capitan High School. Although Joe was not asked to throw much in high school, El Capitan's solid front line and three-deep zone made it vulnerable to the pass, so Joe was told to go to the air as much as possible. No one had counted on the elements, however. Not only did Joe have to contend with El Capitan, but with a torrential downpour and a slippery football. It hardly fazed him. Working the spread formation to perfection—his flankerbacks spread wide—he threw twenty times for more than 220 yards in Granite Hills' convincing victory.

Unlike many of his teammates, Joe accepted football even then as a game and not as a life-and-death proposition. "He was a well-rounded youngster," says Symington, "whose reasons for living did not consist solely of football. He knew he wanted to play football, but he had other interests. He wouldn't break into tears after a bad game like a lot of other kids. Joe would get upset, but he always had the attitude there would be another game. He had this air of confidence about him."

Not only was Joe developing the physical tools of a fine quarterback, but he instilled confidence in his high school team with his poise under fire. In later years, he would show this same maturity both on and off the field.

"In the huddle some quarterbacks can destroy a team just by what they say," notes Symington. "Some are real blah, they just come into the huddle and say you do this, you do that. I never felt that way with Joe. His teammates always felt as if he had everything under complete control. And he usually did."

Joe was soft-spoken and a reporter once asked Paul Hackett whether this would hamper his quarterbacking ability. Hackett gave the same answer as Symington. "You may not think he has the verbal ability to lead a football team," Hackett said, "but when you're around him he has that deliberate confidence. He reeks of knowing where he's going and what he wants to do."

In June, 1973, however, there seemed to be no dearth of fine young quarterbacks coming out of the high school ranks on the West Coast. Joe had several feelers, but upon graduation found himself with no major college scholarship offers. The only four-year school to offer him a free ride was the University of California at Riverside, a school not known for its prowess on the football field. Today, UC Riverside does not even field a football team.

"Most kids would have taken any offer," says Symington. "But Joe always seemed to have a plan for what he wanted to do. As it turned out, it was a smart move."

That move was to go to a junior college. Junior college football in California is nothing to be scorned. The competition is intense and the level of play above that of many smaller four-year schools. Many fine football players, including a running back named Orenthal James Simpson, have spent two years of seasoning at a California junior college before matriculating at a major university.

Joe chose Grossmont Junior College, a school of about sixteen thousand commuting students in the greater San Diego area. Grossmont was competing in the rough-and-tumble Mission Conference then—it has just recently moved up to the even tougher South Coast Conference—and employed a quarterback-oriented offense with heavy emphasis on passing. Joe knew he would receive full exposure at the school and, if he was indeed any good, the big college recruiters would take notice.

75

"I would say that in his first year he was just a very average junior college quarterback," says Jack Miyamoto, the head football coach at Grossmont. "He was always very intelligent and hard-working."

Joe improved during the end of his freshman year, though, and led the team to three consecutive victories. With a rigorous weight training program that spring and summer, he figured to be ready for his second season at Grossmont.

Then, during the spring, he had a mole on his chin removed. It had been giving him some trouble during the football season, the chin strap on his helmet irritating it and causing discomfort. He had had a similar growth removed while he was in high school, but this time, following the advice of the school dermatologist, he had a routine biopsy done. The tissue was found to be malignant.

"His mother and father were in the Dakotas visiting his brother," remembers Miyamoto. "His mother called here to say they had heard about the biopsy and were coming down. I then told Joe his parents were coming to see him. He had no idea. He hadn't heard the results of the test."

Joe immediately underwent an operation for the removal of lymph glands and salivary glands from his neck, then had to wait around in agony for three days as doctors decided whether or not they had to remove half of his handsome face to stop the spread of the cancerous melanoma.

"My whole athletic life passed before me those three days," Roth later told Skip Bayless of the *Los Angeles*

Times. "It made me realize how important it was to be alive. After you beat something as terrible as cancer, the pressures of football are meaningless by comparison."

Less than three years later, when they buried Joe Roth, Father Hunt recalled how the operation had reshaped Joe's life. "He was tested then and he reordered his priorities," says Father Hunt. "That was the strength of Joe Roth. He knew that from then on, all other setbacks were minor, that he would be more concerned about the bigger issue of facing God."

Even though the cancer had been removed, Joe was told by his doctors that a cancer patient could not be assured of having beaten the disease until he had been given a clean bill of health for at least five years.

"He almost died and that really opened his eyes," says his brother, Tom, now a Seattle realtor. "He would never become the typical football player who drinks beer all day and wants everyone to kiss his feet."

Joe bounced back quickly from the operation and returned to Grossmont, where he played right field for Jack Miyamoto's baseball team. He made few waves, though. "He was a strong-hitting right fielder," says Miyamoto. "But he didn't run too well."

That summer, working in the weight room took priority. He worked out daily on the tricep machine, gradually filling out to a solid 185 pounds—ideal weight for a major college quarterback.

"Joe worked his butt off that summer," says Symington, who by then had joined the Grossmont coaching staff. "He worked as hard as any athlete in the weight room. He ran 100-yard dashes. He was starting to fill out and get stronger. He was never aloof, never satisfied. He always kept working at it."

The 1974 football season, Joe knew, would be his showcase year. A good season would interest the major colleges. Another average year would leave him in the same predicament as that following high school. It was now or never.

It was now. Joe Roth led Grossmont to eight wins and two ties and the California state championship. In the first round of the state playoffs, he erased a 14–0 deficit against Santa Rosa by throwing a fifty-yard touchdown pass with no time left in the first half. In the championship game, he riddled Orange Coast with his passes on the way to a 34–17 victory. Joe himself landed on the Junior College All-American team. His success seemed to impress everyone. Everyone, that is, except Joe.

"He remained very quiet and humble," says Miyamoto. "He used to spend his free time studying. He had a lot of friends, but he didn't recruit them."

Joe finished his junior college career with 211 completed passes in 370 attempts for a near sixty percent completion record. He amassed 2,663 yards in the air and threw for twenty-eight touchdowns. Not surprisingly, the college coaches liked what they saw now. Scholarship offers started to pour in from throughout the West: Oregon, Washington, San Diego State, California . . . of them all, the beautiful green campus at Berkeley, split in half by Strawberry Creek, appealed to him most.

"He got real attached to Mike White, who was a real great recruiter and an honest person," says Jack Miyamoto. "He wanted to stay in California and he wanted to play a major college schedule."

The California Golden Bears were looking for a quarterback to replace Steve Bartkowski, their All-American signal caller the previous year, who had been chosen by the Atlanta Falcons as the number one pick in the National Football League draft. "We had Lou Erber recruiting in San Diego and he brought Joe to our attention," says White, who became an assistant coach with the San Francisco Forty-niners. "We then saw him play at Santa Rosa.

"I think our offense, as well as our academic reputation, gave us a big advantage in getting Joe. The University of Southern California and UCLA had young quarterbacks and they didn't take too many junior college transfers. It was just good timing."

Quarterback coach Paul Hackett was impressed by what he saw of Joe in the junior college playoffs. "I just had to see him throw one ball," Hackett says, "and I said, 'That's the guy. He's in a class by himself.' He was absolutely awesome." Joe's medical history? "All we saw," says White, "was a big, healthy kid who had some great ability. It was not a factor at all."

There were few visible signs of Joe's operation. The pink, five-inch scar that hooked around his left ear was covered by his long, golden curls. His face sometimes became puffy due to the five ounces of lymph glands that had been cut away, but that was rare. Joe looked all ready to go.

Nevertheless, as in high school, it took more than

merely walking on campus to get the starting quarter-back job. During spring practice, White designated Joe the second-string signal caller behind Fred Besana, a steadier, less gifted athlete. The decision had come from painful experience. A year before, White had been un-able to decide between Bartkowski and Vinnie Fer-ragamo as his starting quarterback. The resulting con-fusion had upset the team and resulted in Ferragamo transferring to the University of Nebraska, where he was now a star. White did not want a repeat performance.

"Fred [Besana] had been red-shirted the year before and he had a distinct advantage over Joe in terms of ex-perience with our system," he says. "We didn't want to be wishy-washy in our decision. Yet in the back of our minds we hoped that Joe would overtake Fred because of his greater potential. We knew he was the kind of guy who could make the big play for us."

Joe had an adjustment problem of sorts when he first arrived at Berkeley. It was his first time away from home and, "while he wasn't exactly a momma's boy," according to one of his coaches, he had the same trouble adjusting to a new situation that most college freshman have.

In addition, while Joe had the physical talent, he lacked the mental techniques at first to be a starting ma-jor college quarterback. "If they had a passing drill, he would rip it apart," remembers his brother. "But it would be a different story as soon as they had the defense out there against him."

"Joe had come to Cal because of the success of Bart-kowski," notes Hackett. "He knew that a lot of learning

was involved. He was impatient waiting, yet he understood he couldn't learn the system overnight. He accepted the fact that Fred was ahead of him. He realized
he would eventually get to show what he could do. Later,
his biggest concern when he took over the number one
job was how Fred would feel."

With Besana at quarterback, the season started slowly
for the Golden Bears. They played well, but lost to a
tough Colorado squad, 34–27. Against West Virginia,
they were flat and lost again, 28–10. When his team continued to show little life in its third game at Washington
State's new Pullman Stadium, White decided it was time
to make a move. Out went Besana, in came Roth.

Joe promptly hit his speedy flankerback Wesley
Walker with a forty-one-yard aerial to tie the score at
14–14. Thirty minutes later, he maneuvered his team
ninety-five yards downfield and scored the winning touchdown himself on a short quarterback plunge. The Golden
Bears won the game, 33–21, and seemed, at last, on their
way.

The victory earned Joe his first start in a California
jersey. His opponent the next week was undefeated San
Jose State, an early season victor over Stanford. Although he had what would later be considered an average
passing day for Joe Roth, Joe proceeded to impress his
teammates and coaches with his poise.

Behind 24–20 with slightly more than three minutes
left in the game, Joe found himself with a third-and-
twenty-two situation at his own twenty-two-yard line. Instead of panicking and firing upfield, Joe calmly hit All-
American running back Chuck Muncie up the middle.

By the time San Jose's deep backs had had time to recover, Muncie had squirmed his way for twenty-five yards and a California first down. Then on the very next play, Joe fired a pass for twenty-three more yards to Steve Rivera. Two plays later, with a third-and-fourteen on the San Jose State forty-six-yard line, Joe faded back and let fly with a perfect over-the-head, on-your-fingertips strike to Walker for the winning touchdown.

"Roth really showed us something today," said Walker after the game. "He's some quarterback."

"Of course, nobody throws like Bartkowski," said Muncie, "but this guy comes close. Real, real close."

Joe's teammates were impressed by his heroics, but no more so than his coach. White knew then that he would be entering the league part of his schedule with a winning squad and an exciting young quarterback. "A loss would have turned the season around for us," says White, who a year earlier had led California to a 7–3 record. "It became obvious after the San Jose State game that although Besana was the guy we stuck our hat on, Roth was the guy with the great talent."

The next two games, California ran roughshod over conference foes Oregon, 34–7, and Oregon State, 51–24. Since both opponents were weak against the run, Joe kept the ball on the ground—with the result that California received its first national ranking in years: No. 19 in the Associated Press poll. It was a welcome sight for Golden Bear rooters who had suffered through three years of NCAA probation for recruiting violations. The penalty had been exclusion from all national ratings and any post-season bowl game consideration.

Steamrolling now, California charged into UCLA—and lost, 28–14. Although Joe hit seventeen of thirty-seven passes for 226 yards and threw a ten-yard TD pass to Steve Rivera, fast becoming his favorite receiver, UCLA found the California defense moveable, and the loss left California with a 3–1 conference mark. If the Golden Bears were to have any chance at the Pacific Eight title or the trip to Pasadena and the Rose Bowl, they knew they could not afford a second loss.

Unfortunately, USC was next, which was something like getting knocked down by a wave, and struggling back to the surface, only to be approached by a second, even larger wave. Southern California was the No. 4 team in the nation—undefeated and untied—and just about everyone considered it the class team in the conference.

It was then that California was hit by a bit of good luck—or USC by a bit of bad luck, depending on your point of view. The coach at USC was John McKay, a college football institution, like Joe Paterno at Penn State and Bear Bryant at Alabama. Many players had come to USC specifically to play for McKay, and when the news leaked out that he was close to signing a two million dollar pact to coach the Tampa Bay Buccaneers, an NFL expansion team (which he did shortly thereafter), the news did not sit at all well with them. It was as if General George Patton had bid his World War II troops farewell to drill a foreign army. It was almost traitorous.

Whether it was McKay's impending departure or simply the masterful passing of Joe Roth, USC came out flat and California ran away with the game. Millions of television viewers nationwide saw No. 12 in action, as Joe hit nineteen of thirty-one passes for 244 yards, with Muncie running for another 146, topped off by a quarterback sneak that put the Bears on top to stay, 21–14. A final touchdown sewed the game up and gave California its most important victory in twenty-five years.

Suddenly, after the lean years and the time on probation, 1975 was a renaissance year for football on the Berkeley campus. In Sproul Plaza—where only ten years before, radical leader Mario Savio had inflamed mass rallies, and, more recently, demonstrations against the war and racism had ignited the campus—now the talk was all of Muncie and Roth and Walker and the Golden Bears' first real shot at the Rose Bowl since 1958, when they had been led by a barrel-chested quarterback named Joe Kapp.

"This is not a rah-rah campus," said Dave Maggard, the school's athletic director, when asked about the sudden prominence of football. "The campus still looks the same, you can't see any change, but there is an almost quiet kind of excitement."

According to Mike White, Joe Roth had as much to do with that excitement as anything. "Cal had gone through a lot of turmoil and growth. Joe was just what we needed. He represented integrity and he was a good-looking guy. What he did as an athlete and as a person was a hell of a lot more than throw a pass. As good as Chuck Muncie was, he was still a football player. With a guy like Joe, it was different. Berkeley is a complex place and they are not just going to cheer a winner. Joe was nearly a straight-A student who was involved in the church and who enjoyed doing pretty creative things, like pottery. He helped re-establish some tradition at Cal."

One of those traditions was winning. The following week, Joe proved that his performance against USC had been no fluke with an even more spectacular passing game against the University of Washington. In fact, Joe couldn't have afforded anything less. Washington was one of the other four teams battling for a trip to the Rose Bowl, and, with Muncie sidelined with a sore ankle, California's game had to be almost solely in the air against a Washington pass defense rated the best in the conference and fourth best in the nation.

A win was a must—and win Joe did, puncturing the Husky defense with twenty-four passes in thirty-six attempts for 380 yards, a new school record, including touchdown passes of eleven, twenty-three, twenty-two and three yards. Ten times he found Rivera by himself in the Washington secondary, good for 183 yards. Every pass was needed, though, as Cal just barely won, 27–24.

After the game, quarterback coach Paul Hackett was asked if he considered Joe a better quarterback than Vinnie Ferragamo, then leading Nebraska to the top of the college rankings.

"Better than Ferragamo?" asked the jubilant coach. "Hell, before he's through, he'll be better than Bartkowski."

That week, Joe was named the Associated Press offensive player of the week. It constituted a rare double for the university—the previous week Muncie had received the same honor.

Joe had a difficult time understanding the sudden fuss. After all, he was only nine games out of junior college, and now suddenly he was being besieged for interviews by national magazines and out-of-state media.

"I know if I wasn't playing for a school with a passing offense like ours and so many great athletes, they wouldn't think much of me," Joe told reporters after receiving the award. "All this publicity has surprised me, because if a receiver is open, it's not really too difficult to hit him. And ours are open fifty to seventy-five percent of the time."

With the season finale against arch-rival Stanford two games away, there was some fear of a letdown against Cal's next opponent—non-conference Air Force. That worry passed quickly. Although Joe could not quite match his success of the previous week, he still managed to pass the Falcons dizzy in a 31–14 triumph. In that game, Joe hit on thirteen of twenty-four passes for 248 yards, including touchdown passes of sixty-three and thirty-four yards. Then it was time for Stanford.

Stanford and California are natural rivals for reasons other than simple geography. Academically, both schools are among America's finest, their student bodies among the most diversified. They regularly get athletes who care about more than throwing a football or making a tackle, so it is no surprise that Joe Roth was drawn to one of these schools.

"I like it at Berkeley because people are interested in so many things besides football," Joe once said. "That's why I didn't want to go to some other schools which are known virtually as 'football factories.' You're transformed into some kind of a cosmic person there. Sooner or later, I'll quit football. Then how long will the publicity last? Then what will I do?"

This would be the seventy-eighth meeting between the two schools and the first time in many years that the Rose Bowl and the Pacific Eight title would hang in the balance. Both schools approached the game tied with UCLA, all atop the standings with identical 5–1 conference records. If UCLA lost to USC (earlier season victories over California and Stanford gave UCLA the edge if it won), then the winner of the California-Stanford game would own at least half the conference crown and the Rose Bowl berth. The teams girded for the battle.

So did the students. A California-Stanford game is never complete without pranks, so it was not surprising when one morning students on the Berkeley campus woke to find their water fountains sabotaged—instead of water, out spouted "Cardinal"-red Kool Aid—and a sixty-five-foot red-and-white sign with the word "Indians" (Stanford has two nicknames) hung from Berkeley's 397-foot Campanile tower.

California retaliated by tearing down the goal posts on the Stanford freshman field and disrupting the toilet system at a Palo Alto dormitory. On the day of the game, Stanford students countered by placing seven thousand bogus *Daily Californians* with the headline "NCAA Nixes Rose Bowl: Bears Back on Probation" in vending machines on the Berkeley campus.

It was the Golden Bears who got the final laugh, however. In front of 88,000 fans jammed into Stanford's stadium, the top offensive team in the country ran up 488 total yards and overpowered Stanford, 48–15.

California had taken a quick 7–0 lead on a seven-yard pass from Roth to Muncie. Later, after Stanford had closed the gap to 27–15 with less than thirteen minutes remaining, Joe moved the team from deep within its own territory with strikes first to Walker for forty-six yards, then to Muncie for fifteen. Joe's totals for the day: fourteen of twenty-three for 163 yards.

"I'll have to admit I was thinking about the crowd and how it would be in that big stadium with so many Stanford rooters," Joe said in the winning locker room. "I tried to get my mind off it when we had our team meeting, but it wasn't until we got on the field to warm up that I relaxed a bit. That's where our California rooters helped. They really fired us up."

Unfortunately, the season ended on a disappointing note for California when UCLA barely got by USC and received the Rose Bowl berth (and beat Michigan on New Year's Day). Since every other bowl game had been set long before Cal's final contest, the Golden Bears were left out in the cold, No. 14 AP ranking and 8–3 record notwithstanding.

But it had been a triumphant year for Joe Roth. He had equalled Craig Morton's single-season passing record by completing 126 of 266 passes for 1,880 yards and fourteen touchdowns, the best mark in the conference and the eighth best passing record in the country— and Joe had even missed two games. He had led the nation in average gain per completion with 8.4 yards a pass, still a school record, and in fewest interceptions, with seven.

After the season, Mike White said, "Joe's in the same class as Plunkett [the 1972 Heisman Trophy winner] and Bartkowski. He's as cool and as smart and as efficient as any quarterback I've ever been around."

"Joe [has] that great ability to anticipate and release quickly," echoed Paul Hackett. "When he sees that open receiver, bang, the ball's out of his hands and that defensive back had better be ready because it's going to be there."

The experts were ecstatic about Joe's potential. One season—less than nine games—had convinced them that Joe was the finest college passer in the country and a likely first-round pick in the 1977 draft, still a good eight months away.

"We rate Roth the top college quarterback in the country," said Jack White, the San Francisco Forty-Niners vice-president. "He has excellent tools and everything necessary to become a very fine quarterback. He throws an easy ball to catch. He can throw on the move and avoid the rush. And one of the most impressive things about Roth is his poise. I like his size, intelligence and character."

Other NFL scouts agreed. "He's the best pure passer since Bert Jones," said one. "Roth has the ability to be a star in the NFL," said another.

The scouts also liked the training he was getting at California. Unlike most college offenses, White ran a pure pro-style offense with the quarterback dropping straight back ten to twelve yards before he passed, which meant Roth would fit right into the pro ranks.

That summer, Paul Hackett was offered a job at USC, a position with more prestige and greater benefits. The first person he called with the news was Joe.

"I told him I wasn't going to leave because I wanted to stay around for his senior year," recalls Hackett. "He started telling me, 'There is no way you can't go. Professionally it's the best thing for you.' He made the decision a lot easier for me."

That summer, too, talk of the Heisman Trophy began circulating through the hills of Berkeley. Muncie had finished second to Ohio State's Archie Griffin in 1975 and Joe was now being tabbed as the top quarterback in the country. *Playboy* magazine had already picked him as its All-American choice.

Joe himself was pretty cool about the buildup. "I think the Heisman Trophy is just something that comes along if you perform well enough during the course of the season," he reasoned. "I think that it would be a great reflection on our team if I'm able to get the Heisman because these guys would really be part of it."

If Joe had stayed healthy all year, he just might have won it.

How much Joe still thought of his earlier brush with death is not known. He was considered an enigma of sorts on campus and was "categorized as a loner" on the team, according to John McCasey, the school's sports information director.

Some people still on the California campus believe that Joe always considered the threat of the cancer returning a definite possibility. "I think that's why Joe never had a steady girl friend," says McCasey. "He didn't want to get involved with someone for her sake, in case the cancer came back."

Hackett, who smoked cigars with Joe to celebrate the second anniversary of his operation, agreed. "He didn't have many close friends. He thought only a few people could handle all this. I think he knew all along something was going to happen to him. He didn't want to get too close and hurt too many people."

Joe roomed off-campus with John Matlock, a non-football player with whom he had become friendly during his junior year. Unlike some of his flashier teammates, Joe drove around in a beige Volkswagen and dressed with more emphasis on comfort than show. He never drank or smoked. On Saturday nights, he often studied to maintain his 3.0 point average in physical education or listened to his stereo. On Sunday mornings, he attended Mass.

He explained to Matlock that the reason he dated no girl exclusively was because he figured he would be playing professional football in 1977 and he didn't know what city he would be living in. He did not want to get involved with someone, he said, until he knew where he would be. More likely, however, he wanted to wait until he was confident he had beaten the cancer.

"He never spoke of his fears to me, but that fall he suddenly stopped writing to his high school girl friend,

Lynette Elston," says Jim Symington. "It seemed he didn't want to complicate her life. He wanted her to think he was just cooling things down."

That was the kind of person Joe was, says Paul Hackett. "He was absolutely unreal. You had to wonder sometimes if he was putting you on. His kindness as a person, his loving nature, was something else. He was so unselfish, he never talked about himself. His thinking was always, 'What can I do to make you happy?' "

Several people close to Joe believe there was evidence the cancer had reappeared as early as that summer, but by the fall he knew for sure. "It was brought to his attention the week of the third game of the season," Mike White says. "From then on, he lived with this concern. He had to shoulder this all by himself."

California opened its 1976 season against three nationally ranked opponents. Although Muncie had graduated, most experts believed the Golden Bears would be one of the prime competitors for the conference title and the trip to Pasadena.

Before the opening game, Joe was chosen the team's offensive captain. He then went out against the Georgia Bulldogs and threw for 379 yards, only one yard under his school mark. Unfortunately, Georgia had even better success against the California defense, and won, 36–24. The following week against No. 1–ranked Oklahoma, the story was much the same. Joe threw for 284 yards and a touchdown, but the Golden Bears lost again, 46–27. Nevertheless, Sooner coach Barry Switzer came away with stars in his eyes.

"They say that only Joe Namath was better at this

stage and I'm willing to agree with them," Switzer said after the game. "Lord, but this young man can get the ball there and he sets up fast behind the line. His arm is fine, but his feet and perceptions are better. He just gets there, sees his man and throws."

Against Arizona State, which had finished 1975 as the No. 2 team in the country, the Golden Bears won convincingly, 31–22, but something seemed to be wrong with Joe: he hit only ten of twenty-seven attempts for a mere 102 yards. "Before the game," says Tom Roth, "he had become aware that something was wrong. The X-rays had found something."

His statistics were up during the next two weeks. Against an undermanned San Jose State team, beaten 43–16, he connected on sixteen of thirty passes for 229 yards, and in a victory over Oregon, 27–10, he completed eighteen of twenty-eight for 208 yards. Then the season came tumbling down on Joe and Cal. The following week, winless Oregon State beat the Bears, 10–9, and sent Joe to the sidelines with a sprained right knee and ankle. Even before being replaced by Besana, however, he had been off-target, hitting only thirteen of twenty-eight attempts and throwing three interceptions.

Joe never regained his magic, as Cal dropped games to its three California rivals—UCLA, USC and Stanford —and only narrowly defeated Washington and Washington State. In the final season loss to Stanford, he connected on just eleven of twenty-seven passes for 100 yards. Cal finished the year at 5–6.

Joe ended the season with 154 completions in 295 attempts for 1,739 yards, a disappointing year, even though it still put him among the five best passers in the country. A consensus All-American in pre-season, Joe was beaten out for top quarterback honors by Tommy Kramer of Rice. Obviously, Joe had lost something as the season progressed.

Sometime near the end of the 1976 football year, Joe had apparently become fully aware of the fact that he was dying. The melanoma, one of the most virulent forms of cancer, had apparently reached his liver. It was in a stage too advanced to be stopped.

Joe did not want any word of it to get out. He asked White and Maggard to keep the news from reporters. "If anybody asks me, I'll lie," he reportedly said. "I don't want sympathy. I want to play football. I want to be drafted by the pros. I want to be hopeful every minute."

"Joe's brother called the head coach [of Grossmont Junior College] in December and told him that Joe was having problems with his health again," says Symington. "He asked us not to tell anyone. There had been rumors down here about his health. Joe would call us regularly and ask us how things were going. He came back to speak at banquets and he was very appreciative of those who had helped him. He never spoke about himself.

"We look back and figure he must have known then and just wanted someone to talk to. No, he never said he was sick."

Joe was not ready to lie down and die. He wanted to continue playing football.

According to White, no one knew the "finality" of

Joe's condition until more than a month later. Only a select group—the Roth family, White, Matlock and Father Hunt—were aware of how sick Joe was.

"Two weeks after the final game, Joe woke up and found lumps all over him," White recalls. "He went to a doctor and had it looked at and was told the lumps were malignant. We then had other tests performed— liver scan, lung scan, brain and heart scans—and they found a high incidence of the stuff.

"Joe and I went to Dr. Michael Friedman to discuss the possible options. The doctor said it could be a matter of years, months, weeks or days. Joe and his family elected chemotherapy. I was there when they gave him the first treatment and it made him sick as a dog. They inject something and it turns you inside out. He was sick all night."

Joe continued chemotherapy treatments the rest of his life. While the news up to then had been kept out of the papers at Joe's request, many local and out-of-town sportswriters became curious about Joe's health.

"I don't know how he can live with this thing," said teammate Ted Albrechta before the East-West Shrine Game, in an off-the-record interview. "A lot of writers in the Bay Area know the story, but they're sitting on it. They like Joe. He's been a great guy here. His story will probably get out in the next few months or so. I just hope no one around here breaks it."

Joe was scheduled to play in the Shrine Game, but instead decided to visit his parents in Jerome, Idaho, during Christmas vacation. He was starting to look pale and anemic from the disease, but managed to back out of the game without the press becoming too nosey by saying he had back spasms.

The upcoming Hula Bowl in Honolulu and Japan Bowl in Tokyo were different stories, however. Joe was determined to play in both of them, and since Mike White was the West team's coach in both games, he made sure Joe got his chance.

"Dr. Friedman felt it was most important for Joe to live life as normally as possible," says White. "He gave him a blood test before we left for Hawaii just to make sure nothing sudden would happen while we were over there. He gave him a clean bill of health to play."

In Hawaii, life seemed fairly normal for Joe. He surfed several times with his teammates and his room-mate John Matlock, who had been invited by White to accompany Joe on the trip. Joe and Matlock also hit some local discos with White's teenage daughter who, understandably, had a crush on Joe.

Shortly before the game, however, a *Los Angeles Times* reporter broke the story. The news of Joe's fight against cancer burst from newspapers across the country.

"After the story broke, I pulled the squad together and explained what the situation was," says White. "I told them there would be a lot of newsmen around and that Joe should be treated like one of us. I told them there was no timetable or finality to it."

Reached in Hawaii, Joe admitted for the first time that he was undergoing treatment at the University of California Medical Center in San Francisco.

"I don't want to talk about it," Joe told a *San Francisco Chronicle* reporter by telephone. "But I'll say that

I've been having treatments for a few weeks and things are looking good. I've had the stuff before, so it's no big deal for me. I have been medically cleared to play in the bowl game. I feel fine . . . I worked out yesterday and today and I plan to play Saturday."

Fishing for more information, the newspaper contacted a local doctor, who gave some hope to the *Chronicle*'s readers. "It's impossible to know how the disease will affect different people," the doctor said. "Some don't last too long, some live nearly a normal life."

Joe knew there was no hope, however. Dr. Perry Patmont, the team physician, had given Joe the full story at the patient's request, but Joe never revealed his knowledge about the terminal condition, except to his family, priest, roommate and coach.

"I had dinner with him about four weeks before his death," remembers Paul Hackett. "I asked him how he was doing and he said, 'Hack, I'm doing super. The doctors said the treatments are coming alone fine. I'll be down to visit you in a couple of weeks.' Somehow, he kept that bouncy, eternal optimism."

Joe Roth kept the news to himself because the one thing he did not want was sympathy. During his last two months he kept a determinedly low profile in a town where he was one of its biggest heroes.

"I like the cliché about looking at the glass as either half-full or half-empty," Joe said. "I see it as half-full. . . . At least I know what my problem is and how to cope with it. But if everyone starts feeling sorry for me, I'm afraid it will start making me feel the same way. I mean, I fear I won't be the same Joe Roth anymore.

Instead, I'll be Joe Roth, underdog. I don't want that."

Although he was listed at his playing weight of 205, Joe was down to less than 180 pounds for the Hula Bowl, and connected on only four of ten passes in a token appearance. That did not prevent him from insisting on playing in the Japan Bowl, however. Just thirty-five days before his death, he threw for nearly 100 yards, hitting five of six passes.

"In Japan he went on all the tours," says White. "He was on the magazine covers in Tokyo and they all thought here was a big, healthy, blond, All-American kid. Later they found out about his situation and older people came up to him to give him pills and remedies."

The pro football scouts were also becoming aware that Joe did not have long to live. They also knew that Joe normally would be a sure first-round pick—but no team would waste a draft choice on a terminally ill man. Football, after all, is big business.

"I hope the draft is delayed," said one scout late in December, 1976. "Everyone's gonna wonder when the kid's not drafted and then people are going to start calling him. We all know how sick he is. There's kind of a grapevine among scouts."

Up to nearly a week before his death, Joe lived a fairly normal life. He played intramural basketball with a team called the Rejects at the Cal gymnasium. He played golf with White and some Cal recruits. He tossed around a football on the university practice field as late as February 8. By then, he had moved into Mike White's house.

Outwardly, Joe tried to stay as optimistic as possible.

He told White that even if he couldn't play professional football in 1976, he might get a job as a coach until he was cleared to play.

On February 10, Joe entered the UC Medical Center. He stayed a week. Blood clots developed in his legs and doctors told him they would have to amputate to save his life. Instead, he asked to die at home, among his family, friends and teammates.

"In the hospital, he was dying and he wanted to be taken home to die," Hackett says. "But first he wanted to know whether this would be a burden to others."

Joe's parents came in from their Idaho home to see their youngest son for the last time. At Joe's request, they had stayed away until the end.

"Joe didn't fear dying," his father later said. "He didn't complain about the suffering. Most people had given up days earlier. But he didn't like the thought of being disabled. He just wanted to go home—back to his apartment—and die in peace."

Every ninety minutes, Joe was forced to take morphine shots to kill the pain. Members of the football team took three-hour shifts outside his room during the final days. It was tiring and depressing for those who stayed, and there was no indication as to how long he could hold out.

He now weighed little more than 100 pounds. Nevertheless, "he had an air and presence that was staggering at the end," remembers Hackett. "He had grown a beard and he hadn't cut his hair and it was pretty long. He looked almost angelic. Others all around him were breaking down. But not Joe."

Joe even kept making jokes. When Hackett walked in once, Joe said, "Hey, look what I did for this guy. I got him off the recruiting trail." He also apologized for imposing on everyone, especially his sister-in-law and Bonnie Miller, the football team's secretary, who were injecting him with morphine. He asked Bonnie if she wanted to dance.

"He still cracked jokes, but he couldn't smile like he used to," his mother remembers. "That's what I missed most. They warned us that many people in his condition get bitter and say things they don't mean. But not Joe."

On February 19, at 3:55 P.M., he died. "He coughed up some of the stuff in his lungs, took one more breath and that was it," says Bonnie Miller. "We laid him down. And somehow he looked so peaceful."

Just minutes before Joe closed his eyes, Mike White and his wife and Lawrence and Lena Roth walked into Joe's room. Joe's parents had gone out to the Whites' house for a change of scenery.

"As soon as we walked in, he acknowledged all of us," White says. "It was as if he was waiting to say goodbye to those he had been closest to. Then he fell asleep."

Joe's death was announced that night at the California-Washington basketball game in Harmon Gymnasium. Many students wept openly when they heard the news.

On February 22, more than a thousand people filled Newman Hall to pay their final respects to Joe Roth, whose body would be moved to a family plot in Idaho. Among the mourners were relatives, teammates and coaches, as well as students from all over the university who had come to say goodbye to a young man they respected.

"We have all grown older in an instant," said Father Michael Hunt, quoting Daniel Patrick Moynihan's farewell to John F. Kennedy. "We will surely laugh again, but we will never be young again."

Joe's roommate John Matlock described him as "everybody's friend," and tried to introduce a less solemn note. "He sang offkey in the shower," he said, "and he made a great meatloaf."

Matlock later told a reporter, "It's just beginning to sink in how privileged I was to know him as well as I did. From the first time we met, when he was just another football player struggling to make the squad, he never changed. I guess that's why it's tough for me to think of him as anything but plain old Joe."

Hackett called his relationship with Joe Roth the high point of his coaching career, though he had coached other excellent quarterbacks before. "Joe never raised his voice," says Hackett. "He was never demanding. He was inquisitive and he would question things, but he was never forceful in wanting anything. He had a basic belief in people and a confidence that they were good."

The University of California Golden Bears wore black arm bands during 1977 in mourning for Joe. On the bands were three words: Faith, Humility, Courage. These words, according to Mike White, best described Joe Roth.

"He had tremendous religious faith in God—not

101

something he used as a crutch in the end but something he had had his whole life and which gave him great stability," he says.

"In the newspapers they always wanted to write, 'Telegraph Hill Joe,' a takeoff on Broadway Joe [Namath]," White continues. "Joe didn't like that. He would say, 'Just call me plain Joe.' And, of course, his courage began when he found out how sick he was. He never once complained about his illness."

HARRY
AGGANIS

Time passes slowly in West Lynn, Massachusetts.
A factory town a dozen miles north of Boston, West
Lynn is filled with church steeples that dot an otherwise
empty skyline, and rows of gray and white shingled
houses standing like old New Englanders, tired, but
strong. Its people are hardworking, simple and prag-
matic. They learn early that one gets what one deserves,
that the good life is not simply handed over on a silver
platter. They believe in the American ethic, that through
perseverance and toil one can attain almost anything.

Harry Agganis was West Lynn's prodigal son. He
lived his entire life—except for his college years at the
Sigma Alpha Epsilon fraternity—on the second floor of
a small six-room frame house on Waterhill Street, across
the street from a General Electric factory and a meat

packing plant. At the foot of the street is Barry Park, where he threw footballs and hit baseballs.

It is easy today to see the imprint made on West Lynn by its most famous citizen. There is a Harry Agganis Square at the corner of Waterhill Street, an enclosed rock garden only yards from where he once lived. There is a field house and community center and a memorial foundation, all bearing his name. A town like West Lynn does not forget easily.

"The Golden Greek," as he was called to his delight by sportswriters, friends and fans, was a high school superstar, college football All-American and promising major league baseball player. All in twenty-five years.

He was born April 30, 1930, to George and Georgiana Agganis, who had come to America from Loggonike, Greece, shortly after the turn of the century. Harry was the baby, the youngest of seven children, his four brothers, Jimmy, Demo, Philip and Paul all ten years older or more. His father worked as a shoe factory foreman and later as a laborer on one of Franklin D. Roosevelt's WPA projects. The family rented part of their gray-shingled house to bring in additional income.

In the seventh grade, Harry got a job buffing and shining shoes after school for six dollars a week. He quickly moved up to ten dollars a week as a doughnut maker in a bakery. While working was necessary for the family to make ends meet, Harry still had the time to play sports. A left-hander, he tossed footballs and baseballs around dusty Barry Park with neighborhood kids like Billy Porter and George Bullard, both of whom would later play professional baseball. In football,

106

Harry liked to model himself after Sammy Baugh, the great Washington Redskin quarterback of the 1940s. Later, in both high school and college, he would wear Baugh's No. 33.

By the time he was fourteen, Harry was already competing on city championship baseball and football teams at Breed Junior High School and, on Sundays, playing in the uniform of the Lynn Frasers, a local semi-pro team. Some of the teams the Frasers played against were from military bases and featured established major league pitchers serving wartime duty, but that hardly fazed Harry. His batting average was .342.

"He was always a unique kind of guy," remembers Harold Zimman, his high school line coach and later his close adviser. "He was not just a great athlete; he had the ability to make an impact on people."

In 1945, Harry entered Lynn Classical High School, uncharacteristically worried about whether he would make the school football team. He had suffered a broken leg while playing baseball that summer and if the leg hadn't mended properly. . . . He got his answer quickly enough. Scrimmaging as a second-team defensive back, Harry intercepted a pass and headed upfield, only to be suddenly thrown to the ground by a vicious tackle. Getting up slowly, he checked to see if everything was still in its place. He breathed a sigh of relief—the leg had held up just fine.

From that day on, there was no stopping him. In his first season of varsity football, he played most of the year at halfback before coach Bill Joyce shifted him to quarterback, but still managed to finish the season with twenty-eight completions in forty-three attempts for eight touchdowns. He also scored seven touchdowns himself and kicked nine extra points.

Hardly had football season ended, it seemed, when baseball season began. Harry's first varsity year was so good that when the schoolboy-sports editor of the *Boston Globe* was asked to pick the finest schoolboy in the New England area to play on the All-American East squad for a charity game at Chicago's Wrigley Field, he tapped the Lynn sophomore. It was the first time Harry had ever traveled away from the Boston area and, thrilled, he took the train to Chicago with the *Globe* sportswriter and ate peaches and cream for breakfast, hardly his usual diet. In the game itself, the East manager, Pittsburgh Pirate Hall-of-Famer Honus Wagner, put Harry into the game late and he walked in his only appearance at the plate.

Then it was back to Lynn and more football for a one-man show that had the entire Boston area talking. In a season that included eleven victories and one tie, Harry completed 176 of 264 passes for 2,185 yards and twenty-nine touchdowns—astonishing statistics for a high school junior!

The reward was immediate: an invitation for Lynn Classical to come down to Miami and the Orange Bowl to play Granby High School of Norfolk, Virginia, the holder of a thirty-three game unbeaten streak. As scouts from across the country watched, Harry connected on a twenty-one-yard touchdown pass to give Lynn Classical a 21–14 victory and end the streak—all after an opposing player had stepped on his hand early in the game, and injured it.

One of the people watching was the coach of the Boston Yanks of the old Professional Football League. He had been given an ultimatum by the team's owner: find and sign the best T-formation quarterback in the country. After the game, he wailed, "We're going nuts looking for a forward passer, and the best one in the United States is a Lynn schoolboy we can't touch."

Bob Neyland, coach of the University of Tennessee, echoed his judgment. "Agganis could step into any college backfield. That was as fine a job of T-quarterbacking as I've ever seen."

When baseball time came around, Harry once again was picked to play on an all-star team, this time a group called the United States All-Stars who would be playing against a squad of New York City sandlotters. The game was held at the Polo Grounds in New York City, and was the occasion of an unforgettable if embarrassing experience for Harry; one, however, which showed that he could laugh at himself.

"I walked up to the plate and started to get set when a big wave of applause broke out behind me," he told Ed Fitzgerald in an article that appeared in *Sport Magazine* in December, 1952. "Of course, they had just announced my name over the loudspeaker but, for cryin' out loud, I didn't think that was going to cut any ice in New York. So I just kind of ducked my head down and kicked the ground a little with my spikes. Instead of stopping, the applause got louder and louder. Honest, I was blushing.

109

I didn't know what to make of it. I didn't want to be a jerk altogether, so I finally tipped my hat quickly and turned around to look at the stands. There, walking into a front box, was Babe Ruth, waving at everybody and being cheered to the skies. Boy, did I feel like a crumb! It's a good thing everyone was watching the Babe!"

Harry recovered from his embarrassment quickly, however, and returned to Lynn for his final campaign as a high school football star. Already, he was being called the finest schoolboy athlete to play in the Boston area in the last twenty-five years. There were some qualms after the opening game, though, which Lynn Classical lost to Peabody High School, 7–6. Harry had thrown but a handful of passes all game. Had the Golden Greek's magic vanished?

This was one problem Harry was to have throughout college. Gifted with an accurate, hard-throwing left arm, he was still too often hesitant to pass, even though some thought it might be because he did not want to hog the spotlight any more than was necessary.

The coaches quickly set him straight. They told Harry if he didn't start to fill the air with footballs, he would sit. "I told him, 'Look, next week, you'll throw forty passes, ten a period,' " recalls Zimman. "I said, 'Listen, you'll do it because it's in the best interests of the team.' "

Harry got the message the following Saturday. He buried Gloucester High School under an avalanche of passes, hitting twenty-three of thirty-two for 247 yards. Once the fire was lit, Lynn Classical blazed through the final ten games of its schedule.

After the season, the honors came rolling in like driftwood during high tide. The *Boston Herald American* made him the first local boy in history to be named to both the All-Boston area football and baseball teams for two years running. Lynn Classical looked at Harry's 30–4–1 record in three football seasons and promptly retired his No. 33 jersey. His statistics spoke for themselves—326 of 502 passes completed for 4,149 yards, forty-eight touchdowns and thirty-nine extra points.

The Harry Agganis Chowder and Marching Society, which had been founded in his sophomore year, continued to run strong. Later, Harry would have six official fan clubs.

The college recruiters, of course, also came running to look at Lynn's quadruple threat, a man who could pass, run, kick and play defense had the potential to instantly transform a school into a contender. Bill Joyce remembered attending a football clinic in Atlantic City, New Jersey, during Harry's senior year, at which the guest speaker was Notre Dame coach Frank Leahy. After his speech, Leahy walked over to Joyce and said nonchalantly, as if discussing the weather, "I hear you have a pretty good boy up there. Agganis, isn't that his name?" Joyce sent Notre Dame some game films and received a note several days later from Leahy saying, "This boy is the finest football prospect I've ever seen."

Harry had everything a college coach looks for in a football player. At six feet one inch and 190 pounds, the dark, curly-haired Agganis was built like an Adonis, he could run the hundred in ten seconds flat and had an understanding of the game well beyond his years. More than sixty college coaches were ready to give their right arms to add him to their arsenals.

Joyce, of course, was also extremely high on Harry. "I wouldn't swap Harry Agganis for Johnny Lujack," he told a reporter. "Yes, I saw Army and Notre Dame play last year and I saw Lujack break into the starting lineup against Army three years ago, and I still say Agganis can outkick and outpass Lujack right now."

Early in Harry's high school days, however, his father, who was in his seventies, had passed away. Harry had always been close to his mother, and this had put the two on an even more intimate basis. With all of his siblings married and starting families of their own, Harry knew it was his responsibility to take care of his mother. Although schools as different as Dartmouth and Notre Dame beckoned, Harry felt his place was close to home.

"I became close to the boy while he was a senior in high school," says Aldo "Buff" Donelli, who would coach Harry at Boston University. "I knew the things that motivated him and interested him. He had become very, very close to his mother after his father died, and I knew he didn't want to leave the Boston area."

According to Donelli, that quickly limited the competition to Boston University and Boston College. Then John Pappas came on the scene. Pappas, a local business-man who owned controlling stock in Suffolk Downs Racetrack, as well as a number of Italian food stores, had taken an interest in Harry for several years and, as a graduate of Boston University Law School, he is said to have added extra weight to Harry's final decision.

"Pappas told him if he did well in the classroom there would be a job, a good job, waiting for him when he got out," says Donelli. "This made it easier for him to live in Boston without relying upon his mother."

Georgiana Agganis was a woman from the old country. She spoke little English, was plain in appearance, and for years wore only black, in mourning for her dead husband. Yet Harry always made sure she was present at all his big affairs—even if she refused to watch him play football.

"Harry thought she was the Queen of Sheba," recalls Zimman, who now owns a sports publishing firm in Lynn. "When the president of Boston University said to Harry, 'I hear one of the reasons you're coming here is because of your mother,' Harry said, 'Yes, that's right,' and when the president said, 'She must be a terrific woman,' Harry asked if he would like to meet her." So they drove from Boston to Lynn and Harry marched the president right up to the second-floor apartment—which was on the other side of the tracks—and past their black stove to have coffee with his mother. Later, he did the same thing with [Tom] Yawkey, the millionaire owner of the Red Sox."

A story, perhaps apocryphal, is often told to show the sense of self that Harry possessed even then. On the day he announced he would be attending Boston University, the story goes, he turned to Bill Joyce and asked him for a dozen nickels.

113

"What do you need the nickels for?" asked the high school coach.

"Newspapermen," Harry answered. "I promised these guys I'd let them know when I decided what college I was going to."

Harry entered BU in the fall of 1948 and matriculated in the School of Education. Later he would switch to the School of Public Communications, before returning to Education, from which he graduated in 1954. While at BU he became an active member of the Sigma Alpha Epsilon fraternity and served as its pledge master for three years.

As a freshman, Harry's display of self-confidence and awareness of his own ability surprised his college coaches just as much as it had Bill Joyce.

"I was watching the freshman team practice one day and I went over to Harry," comments Buff Donelli, who was then in his second year coaching at Boston University after a short stint at Duquesne University. "I told him there was one pass I wanted him to learn. The pass was the down-and-out, where the receiver goes downfield five or six yards, stops while the defensive man is still running backward, and makes his cut.

"When I told him, he didn't even bat an eye. He looked me straight in the eye and he said, 'Where do you want me to throw it, at his belt or at his shoulder? I was told in high school that throwing it high is a dangerous pass.' I just looked at him. I thought he was pulling my leg."

Harry's freshman career picked up where his high school career had left off. He completed fifty-six percent of his passes that year and ran for a 4.7-yard average. With a student body that was usually somewhat less than enthusiastic about football, more than twenty thousand fans turned out for the BU–Holy Cross *freshman* game.

The next year, well schooled in the T-formation thanks to high school, Harry moved right into the varsity starting quarterback role, replacing senior John Toner, and wasted little time in proving himself. In his varsity debut against Syracuse University, Harry hurled two touchdown passes in an upset 33–21 victory over the Orangemen. The following week he threw three touchdown passes and ran in a fourth score in a 40–21 triumph over Colgate University in upstate New York. On October 15 he met his toughest opponent so far in West Virginia, considered to have one of the strongest teams in the East. It was also to be Harry's homecoming game and the fans filled Fenway Park to overflowing.

"The first time we got the ball," Donelli recalls, "Harry called a handoff to the halfback going to the left. We were on about our own thirty-five-yard line. Without saying anything to anyone, however, he decided to keep the ball. He ran it all the way down to the West Virginia four-yard line. We went on from there and beat the hell out of them."

Playing less than three quarters, Harry threw for three touchdowns and scored one himself in an easy 52–20 decision.

New York University fell next, then Scranton, as Harry set a Boston University record that still stands by connecting fourteen times in twenty-five attempts for 218 yards and a total of four touchdown passes. The next victims were the Owls of Temple University, 28–7. Mid-way through the game, Donelli sat Harry down because he didn't think his star was passing enough.

"Look, coach, we're leading, aren't we?" Harry said. "We'll win this game. I know what I'm doing." Donelli shrugged his shoulders and sent him back in. "Trouble is, he usually does know what he's doing," the coach said after the game. "Sometimes I'm ready to send in a sequence of plays for Harry to use, and before I've had a chance to get to him, he's already called the first play of the sequence I had in mind."

Harry had his own theory about passing, as he told a magazine writer. "There is no point in passing unless you are certain the pass will be caught," he said. "An incomplete pass is just another down, and an intercepted pass is disastrous."

With a perfect 6–0 slate, Boston University had a shot at national recognition the following Saturday against the University of Maryland. Coach Jim Tatum's Terrapins were big and strong, third in the nation in defense, and only a 14–7 loss to powerful Michigan State had marred an excellent year. On game day, Fenway Park was packed with 30,263 fans, almost all of them pulling for the scarlet and white Terriers of Boston University. Boston had never before (or since) been so close to reaching the top.

For most of the game it really looked like Boston University was going to pull it off. Unable to stop Agganis, who ended up completing eight of twelve passes, the Terps found themselves trailing 13–7 late in the second half before finally pulling themselves together, marching

116

down the field and scoring the touchdown and extra point that put them ahead. They held off a late BU surge and won, 14–13. Harry left the field in tears.

Although the disheartened team lost again the following week to St. Bonaventure, 19–0, 1949 still stood as the school's finest year ever in football. Harry had performed sensationally, hitting 55 of 108 passes for fifteen touchdowns—and intercepting fifteen passes on defense to lead the nation. He punted for an amazing 46.5-yard average and ran for an average of 5.4 yards a carry.

For all his success in football, however, Harry still hadn't forgotten baseball. In his first year on the varsity, playing first base, he made the All-New England team (as he would again in 1952) by contributing a .350 batting average and a half dozen home runs. That summer, he joined the Augusta (Maine) Millionaires, a semi-pro baseball team sponsored by the Boston Red Sox. At the time, the Millionaires had twenty-nine alumni playing organized baseball.

Agganis and the other players were paid while they played, working sporadically at an Augusta shoe factory—an excuse to make some money and stay eligible for college ball at the same time—while barnstorming through the state of Maine with an eighty- to ninety-game schedule. They played other semi-pro teams like Lewiston-Auburn and Portland, as well as town teams, including a squad of local prison inmates.

Ted Lepcio, who later became one of Harry's teammates on the Red Sox, was an infielder on the Millionaires, and he and Agganis became close friends.

"We roomed together for three years," says Lepcio,

now a trucking executive. "Harry was an extremely loyal, good friend. He was always strong in his opinions. He was vocal, for instance, when he thought he should be playing.

"He was a great comic, always full of hell. At Augusta, we were all a bunch of crazy college kids. I remember once we were staying at a small hotel and Harry instigated a watermelon fight. The town police kicked us out of the hotel and we almost spent the night in jail."

Harry had a more serious side too, though. That spring he and Harold Zimman watched Babe Didriksen Zaharias, the greatest woman athlete of all time, win her final professional golf tournament on a Peabody, Massachusetts, golf course. Babe had recently undergone cancer surgery and would die soon after. The sight sobered Harry. To think of all that ability gone to waste. . . . "Harry felt he had a great rapport with her," Zimman says now.

A Marine Corps reservist since the summer of 1948, Agganis' number came up while he was practicing for his junior season. A week or so later, he exchanged his scarlet and white Boston University jersey for Marine khakis. Buff Donelli was distraught. By drafting Harry, the Marines had destroyed Boston University's football hopes in 1950.

"How do you feel," one reporter asked. "How do I feel?" Donelli yelled. "Did you ever have an attack of appendicitis and then get hit on the head by a sledgehammer? The guy is only the greatest quarterback in the business, that's all. I said it when he was a freshman

118

and I'll say it again. Only once in a lifetime a Baugh or a Luckman or an Agganis comes along. How do I feel?"

Life at Camp Lejeune, North Carolina, was not too bad for Harry. He was placed in the camp's athletic department, where he played an eleven-game football season against college teams and other service squads, some comprised of professional talent. The camp also had an eighty-game baseball schedule. Harry batted .347 and led Camp Lejeune to a fourth-place finish in the National Congress Championship Tournament in Wichita, Kansas.

Times, however, were rough back home for Harry's mother. Although Harry sent nearly all his pay to her, she still had trouble making ends meet, so, with the promise from John Pappas of a job in the public relations department at Suffolk Downs, Harry filed for a dependency discharge from the Marines. They granted it on September 20, 1951; Harry hustled back to Boston, and that week was in uniform calling signals for Boston University in its opening season game against William and Mary College.

Even with only two days of practice, Harry performed well enough that day to hit on ten of twenty-three passes for two touchdowns. But the Terriers lost, as they did again the next week, before evening their record by beating Louisville and Harry's alma mater, Camp Lejeune. It looked like BU was back on track, but even so, the prospects against the following week's opponent looked grim. College of the Pacific, larger, faster and much more powerful, was ripping through its opponents on the West Coast.

"They're the greatest team to play here in ten years," said Coach Donelli; "I truthfully can't see how we can beat them."

But beat them they did. Even though College of the Pacific arrived in Fenway Park undefeated in 1951, averaging two hundred yards per game with a team from which no less than eight players would move on to the pros, Agganis put on one of his finest football displays. He started early by intercepting a pass at his own goal line to thwart a Pacific threat, then went on to complete sixteen passes in twenty-four attempts for 174 yards, in an overwhelming 27–12 triumph.

"Their coach [Ernie Jorge] came over to me afterward," Donelli recalls, "and told me if it wasn't for Agganis. . . . He just couldn't get over the performance the guy put on."

But that's what coaches and writers throughout the country were saying. Boston University was riding high on the golden left arm of Harry Agganis.

After Harry picked apart the University of Oregon by throwing for two touchdowns in a 35–6 victory, a scout for the University of California said, "Agganis is the best T-formation quarterback I have ever seen. I scouted Oregon three times this season and discovered three principal weaknesses. Agganis found and exploited them all in the very first series."

Even with a so-so 6–4 season, many called Harry the finest quarterback in the nation. At season's end, he had completed 104 of 185 passes for 1,402 total yards, fourteen touchdowns and a terrific 56.2 percentage, second in accuracy only to future pro Babe Parilli of the University of Kentucky. Once again, he had punted for a forty-yard average.

"He moves back slowly from his position behind the center, calmly looks the situation over, and if his line holds, takes his time about getting the ball away," wrote Al Hirshberg in an article that appeared in *The Saturday Evening Post* on October 18, 1952. "If it doesn't, Harry dances back and forth, shaking off opposing linemen until he finds either a suitable receiver or a hole through which he can run. If he is really swamped by a wave of tacklers, he relaxes and goes down gracefully. 'He eats the ball,' an observer remarked, 'as though he liked the taste.' "

Dick Kazmaier of Princeton won the Heisman Trophy in 1951, but many felt the award should have gone elsewhere. "Kazmaier," said Donelli bluntly, "can't carry Agganis's shoes."

Harry did win the Bulger Lowe Award, however, given annually to the top athlete in New England. Not surprisingly, he was named Boston University's top athlete for the second time.

The best estimation of Harry's talent, however, was the decision by the Cleveland Browns to draft him first in the year's college grab bag. Harry had another year of college football remaining, but was eligible for the draft since his original class had graduated.

The Browns were looking for a replacement for their great but aging quarterback, Otto Graham. Paul Brown, the Browns' head coach, figured it would be best to draft Harry right away and then talk with him during his senior year, so that in June he would be ready to sign with the Browns. In addition, it was rumored that the Pittsburgh Steelers would be ready to grab him if Cleveland didn't.

In Boston, the debate began in earnest on whether Harry should sign with the Browns after his senior year at BU or play baseball—all sixteen major league teams were said to be after him.

"He can make more money playing football," Donelli told a reporter. "He's the most remarkable forward passer I have ever seen. The kid can last forever. He'll never have to go into the sticks if he plays football."

Bill Joyce, his old coach at Lynn Classical High School and a scout with the Boston Red Sox, saw it another way. "He's had the equivalent of two years of minor league ball already," Joyce told *The Saturday Evening Post*. "He's playing with boys who are in the majors now. He'll be there within a year. Money? How high can the Cleveland Browns go? The cash potential in baseball is unlimited."

Donelli put up a brave front, but deep down he knew that Harry's last season on the gridiron would be in 1952.

"He was the complete [football] player," Donelli says now. "If not *the* greatest punter in the country, he was one of the greatest. He was a great defensive man. He could have made it in the pros as a running back, for he had a natural change of pace and could probably run the hundred in ten seconds or better. But I was not surprised that he picked baseball. He loved the Red Sox. [Ted] Williams was there and he absolutely idolized him. I was hoping he would take football. I thought he would hit football stardom real quick."

Before Harry could sign with either the Browns or the Red Sox, however, he still had one more year of college football to go. Perhaps Harry was distracted, perhaps this just wasn't the team's year—in any case, it was a disappointment. Although Harry still managed to throw for 766 yards and five touchdowns by completing 226 of 418 passes, the team finished at 5–4–1. One low and one high point stood out from the season.

Against the No. 2–ranked Maryland, the Terriers were playing competently when, early in the second quarter, Harry dropped back to pass and was pounced on by a mountain of charging Terrapins. Harry was gingerly removed from the game and transported to a hospital with a serious rib injury. The Terriers proceeded to go down quietly to defeat, 34–7.

Harry promptly checked himself out of the hospital, determined to play the following week, but, climbing into his jersey the day of the game, the pain became worse than ever. "He looked like a ghost," Donelli says. He sat out that contest, but later played against Villanova in a losing cause, wearing a plastic cast around his chest.

The high point of the season occurred on October 11 against the University of Miami, listed by the bookmakers as a four-touchdown favorite. Harry was literally all over the field that day in a 9–7 victory. He connected on four consecutive passes that resulted in BU's only touchdown; booted punts of fifty-eight, sixty-five and sixty-seven yards, the final kick resulting in the winning safety; made fourteen tackles and intercepted two passes.

One final football note remained when, on January 3, 1953, along with the other top players in the country, Harry participated in the Senior Bowl game in Mobile, Alabama. Any lingering doubts about Harry's football prowess were put to rest as Harry dueled with All-American quarterback Jack Scarbuth of the University of Maryland, one of the men who had been instrumental in the Terrapins' whipping of BU two months before. Revenge was sweet. Harry showed he had completely recovered from the rib injury by completing nine of seventeen passes for two touchdowns and kicking two extra points in a 28–13 victory for the East. Playing fifty-nine minutes, he was named the Most Valuable Player of the game. Paul Brown, head coach of the East squad that day, told Harry after the game, "Anytime you want, you can be my first-string quarterback."

Harry, however, had already made up his mind. Two months before, he had officially turned down the offer the Cleveland Browns had been waving at him, and signed with the Red Sox for a $60,000 bonus. Three other major league clubs were believed to have offered him as much money or more.

"It was a question of loyalty with Harry," Zimman says. "He felt he had made a commitment to Joyce. He listened to other offers, but I'm sure he was going to sign with the Red Sox. He knew Joyce would have been embarrassed if he went elsewhere."

Signing with the Red Sox was a dream come true for

Harry. As a high school student, he had nourished his love for the Sox when he took batting and fielding practice at Fenway Park at the invitation of the management. He was especially close to Ted Williams, by then well established as perhaps the finest student of hitting ever to play the game. Williams always took the time to chat with Harry when he drilled with the club.

"Of course I hate to give up football," Harry told reporters after his Senior Bowl triumph, "and I appreciate all the nice things everyone said about my playing, but I realized I couldn't do both. I made my choice when I decided to play baseball with the Red Sox and I'm going to concentrate on trying to make good with Boston."

The Browns were not completely convinced. After all, Harry might *not* make it with the Red Sox. They kept after him . . . just in case.

One day during Harry's first year of spring training, he was warming up in the field when Red Sox General Manager Joe Cronin leaned over to Buff Donelli sitting in the stands. Cronin was complaining about Harry's throwing.

"He has a goddamn football arm," said Cronin. "The muscles in his shoulders are so damn tight."

Donelli shook his head and said, "I tell you, in a year, Joe, he'll be doing everything like everyone else on your club, only a little bit better."

Donelli had no doubts about Harry succeeding in baseball. "He always liked a challenge," Donelli says now. "He had a dogged, inquiring approach to any problem. He would have been a success in any field because he'd fight to overcome any obstacles. In addition, he had a very experienced approach to sports. His nature was to go where the information was available. Sports was his whole life." Donelli sat back in the stands to enjoy.

Harry spent the 1953 baseball season with the Louisville Colonels, the Red Sox minor league affiliate in the American Association, and had a solid year, batting .281, hitting twenty-three home runs and driving in 108 runs.

The Red Sox expected it. On signing Harry in 1952, they had sent first baseman Walter "Moose" Dropo to the Detroit Tigers in a five-player swap—which is not to say the first base job was handed outright to Harry. Dropo, who had been a main cog in the Red Sox attack in 1950 and 1951, had been supplanted by Dick Gernert in 1952. Gernert had held on to the job since, and he was not about to give it up without a fight.

Harry, however, had several things working in his favor. On a team that included such all-stars as Ted Williams, Jackie Jensen, Frank Sullivan and Grady Hatton, Harry was unique—he was the lone homegrown boy. Cronin and manager Lou Boudreau knew that Red Sox fans would like to see their boy in the starting lineup. In addition, Harry had "worked like a dog on his fielding since he was signed," according to Ted Lepcio. Gernert was not a slick fielder.

Gernert's advantages, however, included his experience and the dimensions of Fenway Park. Gernert already had two major league seasons of more than one hundred games each under his belt, and at the age of

126

twenty-four, was only a few months older than Harry. Also, Fenway Park was known to be murder on left-handed hitters like Harry.

Fenway Park is the second oldest park in the major leagues, next to Chicago's Comiskey Park. While stadiums in New York (Ebbetts Field and the Polo Grounds), Pittsburgh (Forbes Field), Detroit (Briggs Stadium), Philadelphia (Connie Mack Stadium) and Cincinnati (Crosley Field) have gone the way of time, and others like Yankee Stadium have undergone major renovation, Fenway has remained untouched.

Located on Yawkey Way (recently renamed after late Sox owner Tom Yawkey) off Boylston Street in downtown Boston, Fenway Park has a character all its own. While left-handed pull hitters have to contend with the 420 feet of open territory in right center and the 380 feet in right, the right-hander faces no such problems. Left field, also known to American League pitchers as the Green Monster, is listed as a mere 314 feet from home plate. Recent measurements, however, show it to be even eleven feet shorter.

What this means is simple. A pop fly that would be easily caught in a more capacious ballpark suddenly has a chance to drop over the fence at Fenway. On line drives, the left fielder suddenly finds himself running out of space and forced to play the ricochet off the wall. By the same token, lefty swingers can easily become frustrated hitting 400-foot fly balls. No wonder the Red Sox prefer right-handed batters.

In fact, until 1954 only two left-handed hitters had played more than one hundred games for Boston since

Tom Yawkey had purchased the team in 1933. Billy Goodman, a popgun hitter, was one. The other was Ted Williams, the Splendid Splinter.

"I'm afraid of what that big right field will do to Harry," said one Red Sox fan. "He's no Ted Williams."

Gernert's 1953 statistics were a perfect example of what the Green Monster can do for a right-handed batter. In Fenway Park, Gernert batted .280, hit sixteen home runs and drove home forty-five runs; in nearly the same number of trips to the plate in the seven other American League ballparks combined, his batting average was .215, with only five home runs and twenty-six RBIs.

Harry outplayed Gernert during spring training, but was on the bench opening day against the Philadelphia Athletics. On April 15, however, Harry broke into the starting lineup against Bob Porterfield, a veteran right-hander who had won twenty-two games the previous year with the Washington Senators. Harry grounded out his first time up; then, in the third inning, he got around on a Porterfield fastball and smacked a long triple to right to drive in the first run of the game. He proceeded to score on a two-run homer by catcher Sammy White. Harry was on his way.

The 1954 Red Sox were not, however. They had plenty of hitting—as usual—but not nearly enough pitching—again, as usual—to keep pace with the league's top teams. While Williams had his usual great year—.345, twenty-nine home runs and eighty-nine RBIs—and Jackie Jensen had twenty-five homers and 117 RBIs, only Frank Sullivan at 15–12 and Tom Brewer at 10–9 sported winning pitching records.

Finishing the season at 69–85, the Red Sox were a sorry fourth, forty-two games behind the high-flying Cleveland Indians, and trailing the Yankees and the White Sox as well. Manager Boudreau was dismissed at the end of the season.

But it had been a pretty good first year for Harry. He had played 132 games to only fourteen for Gernert. At bat 434 times, he had had 109 hits, including thirteen doubles, eight triples and eleven home runs for a respectable .251 average. He had also led the league in assists for a first baseman with eighty-nine.

Although he was no longer the star as he had been at BU, he accepted the change in his role easily.

"We were both young fellows at the time," recalls Lepcio, who played most of the year alongside Harry at second base. "It was different than it is today, where kids are pretty much playing against kids. A lot of the guys on the team had just returned from the service and were older than us. We were kids playing with men and we conformed to the pattern and the structure of the team."

Although he was now drawing a big salary, and the days of shining shoes for six dollars a week had long since passed, Harry continued to live with his mother in their small house on Waterhill Street. He wanted to buy her a bigger house in a nicer area, but Georgiana Agganis, well into her seventies, refused. She told him that she was too set in her ways and that moving to Newton or Marblehead or some other nice surburban area was not for her.

"Maybe it stemmed from his modest upbringing, but

he kind of sensed there were better things in life," Zim-man says. "He liked to wear nice clothes and drive a nice car. He always used to say, 'I want to live nice, I want to live nice.' "

That first year, Harry was closest to Lepcio and Sam Mele, a well-traveled first baseman–outfielder and later manager of the Minnesota Twins, but there was no doubt he was on good terms with everyone on the club. Many of his teammates were invited to Waterhill Street for homecooked Greek meals.

"I would go to a show with him one day and the next day he'd be looking for someone else and it would be that way all the time," recalls Milt Bolling, the Sox third baseman. "He was strictly an extrovert. And he made a lot of friends as a result."

Ted Williams, not one to dole out idle praise, once told a reporter that the rookie from West Lynn had ex-cellent potential. "He needs more experience," cautioned Williams, then thirty-six. "He has to learn how to lay off bad pitches and to hit at a ball on the outside of the plate. Once he learns these things, he has the ability to be a good hitter."

The season over, Harry rejoined Buff Donelli at Boston University that fall to work with the team as a quarterback coach. Only a few months before, in June, he had received his college diploma in physical educa-tion, dashing up Commonwealth Avenue after a game at Fenway Park to pick it up.

There were other things on his mind that off-season as well. From his birth, Harry's parents had inculcated him with a strong Greek identity, and one of the first things he did was start a scholarship for boys and girls of Greek descent at Boston University, which is still going strong. He also gave money from a testimonial in his honor to the small town in Greece where his parents had been born so it could buy sports equipment. In gratitude, the King and Queen of Greece themselves sent him one of his most treasured trophies—an olive wreath.

In addition, he had not entirely forgotten about football, nor football about him. Although he was confident of his baseball ability, in 1954 he signed a contract with the Red Sox that included a clause that would give him the right to try professional football. Shortly before then, his rights had been acquired by the Baltimore Colts.

"Carroll Rosenbloom [then the owner of the Colts] was romancing Harry every time he came to Baltimore," says Zimman. "He would take him out to dinner, to a show, whatever. Harry told me he wanted to be the first to play both professional baseball and football at the same time." Rosenbloom never got to see Harry in a Colt uniform, but he did find a pretty decent quarterback by the following year—John Unitas.

Such activities and ambitions notwithstanding, Harry knew his first responsibility was to the Red Sox. Having slumped somewhat at the end of the 1954 season, Harry spent the winter building himself up to about 220 pounds to prepare for the grueling 154-game schedule.

He also knew he would have some competition for his job. It was not enough that he had bumped Gernert into oblivion the year before; he now had to compete with a pro named Norm Zauchin, who was returning after four years in the service.

As it turned out, Zauchin started the season, but Harry replaced him after several games. The competition between the two men was all on the field, however. They were good friends, often rooming together on road trips.

"I don't root against Norm," Harry said shortly before his death. "I'm not fighting him. He's my roommate and he's a good ballplayer. There's a place in the big leagues for both of us."

The Red Sox were again going nowhere in the American League standings, but Harry was hitting the ball well through the months of April and May. "He was really settling in to enjoy some longevity with the Red Sox," says Ted Lepcio. "He would have played a long time."

On May 16, however, an off-day in the schedule, Harry came to Fenway where several of his teammates were taking batting practice. Mike Higgins, the new Red Sox manager, asked Harry what he was doing at the park, since it was usually only those in batting slumps who turned up then.

In the previous day's doubleheader, Harry had slammed five hits, including a double and triple, against the Tigers. He was batting .300.

"Oh, I have a slight pain in my side," Harry complained mildly to Higgins.

"It couldn't be from your hitting," laughed Higgins. "But go have the trainer look at it."

Jack Fadden, the Red Sox trainer, gave Harry a rubdown and checked his temperature. It was high and Fadden immediately made hospital arrangements for Harry. The doctors diagnosed the ailment as viral pneumonia in his left lung and kept him in the hospital for ten days, but there was nothing unusual about the disease. Treated and released, he was at Fenway Park one hour later to work out.

"I was going good when I got sick," Harry said about his fast convalescence, "and I want to get in there as quickly as I can to get my job back."

Harry was worried about Zauchin taking over again at first base, and he wasted no time returning to the lineup. In hindsight, it is not known whether Harry's quick return had any effect on his fatal relapse. "I remember Sam Mele and myself telling him he was crazy to go on the trip to Chicago," Ted Lepcio says. "But Harry said he was going stir crazy and felt he could help the team by playing."

His hot bat did not cool down in Chicago. On June 2, he singled in the first inning and doubled in the sixth, but on reaching second base, he knelt down, as if in pain. He would not talk about the incident after the game.

He continued to hit the ball hard the next day. Late in the game, with Boston trailing 4–2 and men on base, Harry hit a hard line drive to right field. Jungle Jim Rivera, the Chicago right fielder, got an excellent jump on the ball and picked it off the grass for the out.

The shoestring catch squelched the Red Sox rally and cost them the game. Afterward, a reporter for the *Boston*

Herald American described Harry Agganis as "down." The catch by Rivera dropped Harry's batting average to .313. It would be his final appearance at the plate.

Following the game, Harry began to get back pains. Perhaps hoping that the ache would disappear overnight, he did not tell Jack Fadden about it until the next day in Kansas City. Fadden, however, realizing how sick Harry was, sent him home by plane. Cronin met him at the airport and drove him to Sancta Maria Hospital. The Red Sox placed him on the sixty-day voluntary retired list.

The most anyone expected was that Harry might be forced to miss the rest of the season. At no time was there any reason to think that the disease could be fatal. The word from Dr. Eugene O'Neill, one of Harry's physicians, was "that Harry began playing too soon after his first hospitalization and that this time he'll wait longer before being returned to the active list."

For the next few weeks, doctors reported that Harry was making slow progress from a severe pulmonary infection complicated by phlebitis in his knee, and so no visitors were allowed except for his family. Many of his teammates tried to see him, but were turned away at the door. Norm Zauchin tried unsuccessfully to see Harry three times. Mike Higgins resorted to talking to Harry three or four times a week by phone.

During the end of June, Harry appeared to be feeling better, and could see more people. Harold Zimman and his wife Helen dropped by on June 26. "He wasn't down," Zimman later told reporters. "He'd had phlebitis in his knee for some time and he had had a bad night Saturday. But Sunday he was feeling much better."

Agganis and the Zimmans watched Ed Sullivan's "Toast of the Town" on television and laughed at comedian Bob Hope's antics. While Harry's spirits were good, Zimman said, it became obvious he was perspiring heavily. "Being sick is an education," he remembered Harry telling him. "It gives you a better sense of values."

Harry was hoping to see his old Boston University coach that weekend. It seemed like he was over the biggest hurdle.

"Friday afternoon, he called me," Buff Donelli recalls now. "He had suffered a setback and this was the first day he was feeling right. He called me and said, 'I'm feeling pretty good; why don't you come over?' I could tell he was feeling real good—he started the conversation by calling out old football signals.

"I told him that everyone else would probably be there over the weekend and that Monday morning I'd come and we'd have a good long talk. I told him there were things I wanted to talk to him about and he agreed that Monday would be a good time. And by God, we never reached it. Everything was fine, and bang, he's gone."

On June 27, the late edition of the *Boston Globe* carried the front page headline, "Harry Agganis Dead." He had died at Sancta Maria Hospital shortly past 11:00 A.M. that day, of a massive pulmonary embolism; a blood clot had blocked an artery. Later, friends would wonder what he had been doing at a small convalescent home all that time instead of being in one of Boston's major hospitals.

"I had just seen him the night before and he was looking reasonably well," remembers Ted Lepcio. "He looked to be in no impending danger."

The Boston Red Sox had just arrived at the Schenley Hotel in Pittsburgh, scheduled for an exhibition game that night. Road secretary Tom Dowd was called to the telephone. Ashen-faced, he returned to tell Harry's teammates, "Gentlemen, I have to give out the worst news I have heard since I became road secretary with the Red Sox. Harry Agganis is dead."

The body of Harry Agganis lay in state for two days at St. George's Greek Orthodox Church in Lynn. More than twenty thousand people filed past to pay their last respects. Twenty thousand more lined the one-and-a-half mile route to Pine Grove Cemetery, overlooking Manning Bowl, the scene of Harry's high school triumphs. Harry was buried next to his father.

Harry Agganis has not been forgotten. There is a stadium at Camp Lejeune that bears his name. There are portraits of him in both the baseball and football Halls of Fame. At one time, there was a move to change the name of Fenway Park to Harry Agganis Field.

In a recent poll of Boston sportswriters, Agganis was chosen over the likes of Ted Williams, John Havlicek, Carl Yastrzemski and Bobby Orr as the greatest local athlete of all time.

"In life, Harry Agganis was the perfect model for the

great American sports novel," wrote George Sullivan in
a recent Boston University football program. "In death,
he was the ironic portrait of a Greek tragedy. . . . He
was the Homeric hero, dead at barely 26."

ERNIE DAVIS

THIS IS HOW BEN SCHWARTZWALDER, A GRUFF EX-PARA-trooper from the hills of West Virginia, and coach of the Syracuse University football team for a quarter of a century, remembers Ernie Davis:

"He was so good, he had no imperfections," says Schwartzwalder. "He was like a man with a halo. No one ever had a bad word to say about him. He was close to everyone, always patting everyone on the back. He was such a good kid."

Ernie Davis was also a tremendous football player, one of the finest to ever play in the college ranks. He led Syracuse University to the very top of the football heap and became the first black man to win the Heisman Trophy. Later, he became the National Football League's wealthiest rookie—and the young man who stirred the nation with his smile and courage in the face of death.

139

The Ernie Davis story began in the small town of New Salem, Pennsylvania, on December 14, 1939. Shortly thereafter, his parents were separated. His mother, Marie, moved to Elmira, New York, and his father, whom Ernie never knew, died in an accident. One-year-old Ernie was sent to Uniontown, Pennsylvania, to live with his grandmother and her children until Marie established herself. He spent ten years there.

At the time, the Uniontown area fairly bustled with well-known athletes—men such as Stan Musial, the great St. Louis Cardinal outfielder who lived in nearby Donora, and Johnny Lujack, the famed Notre Dame quarterback from Connellsville.

Ernie was bitten early by the sports bug. At the age of eight, he hiked over four miles for tryouts with Benson's Midget League baseball team, often walking with his good friend Sandy Stephens, who a dozen years later would become an All-American quarterback with the University of Minnesota Gophers and Ernie's competitor for the Heisman Trophy.

The quick reflexes, broad shoulders and fast-moving feet which would be Ernie's trademark in college, however, had not quite arrived at age eight. Ernie made the team, comprised of boys eight to twelve years old, but only as the fifteenth and final man on the squad. Not only that, but on the day the Midget League paraded through the center of town, there was a mixup and Ernie did not receive a team uniform as promised. Holding back the tears, he marched in civvies while his teammates all wore the team colors.

It was not an illustrious beginning to his career.

However, he quickly made up for lost time at the age of eleven when he was at last able to move back in with his mother and her new husband, Arthur Radford, in Elmira.

Elmira had a population of about fifty thousand back then. It was more like a town than a city: nearly everyone knew each other, and Ernie, his mother and stepfather lived in a comfortable two-family house they shared with the Stark family on Lake Street. The old Elmira Free Academy School was just across the street.

Marty Harrigan, the high school's football coach, first laid eyes on the eleven-year-old Ernie when Davis became the new star of the local Pop Warner, or "Small Fry," team. "I heard about this gangly, skinny kid who appeared to be gifted," says Harrigan now. "I didn't know his family—his mother wasn't a local girl—so one Sunday I went out to see him."

Harrigan was not disappointed. By this time, Ernie did have the beginnings of the dazzling footwork and speed that would later make him a star in high school and at Syracuse University. However, when Ernie got to high school, it was in basketball that he made his mark first. At fifteen, he was a solid six feet one inch and 175 pounds, and he became one of the first freshmen ever to make the Elmira Free Academy varsity team. In his very first game, even though he wore a light cast on his left wrist, courtesy of a recent junior varsity football injury, he came in to score twenty-two points.

With Ernie Davis, the Elmira Free Academy basketball team became one of the top teams in the state, at one point reeling off fifty-two straight victories. Ernie himself made both All-State and high school All-American his last two years, but soon his football abilities put even his basketball successes in the shade. While at Elmira Free, Ernie led Coach Harrigan's squad to several championships, and missed a perfect record by only one game, once going so far as to score on two touchdown runs of more than ninety yards apiece.

"He used to grab the football like it was a loaf of bread," remembers Harrigan. "But he had great acceleration and could stop on a dime. Every time it was tough out there—say, when it was 6–6—Ernie was great." Coach Harrigan also points out that while Davis had great physical talents, he had even greater desire. He worked hard to achieve excellence. "When you get talent plus intensity, you get a horse. I remember when Ernie couldn't do a pushup. He had a big set of legs and a great big rump. He developed his torso through a weight program. Later, when he would do five pushups, he'd have the biggest grin on his face you ever saw."

It was the same in the classroom. "He wasn't the greatest student in the world," says Harrigan, "but he prepared himself for college. He worked hard and he made eighties."

People in Elmira remember Ernie Davis not only as a superb athlete, but as a quiet and modest young man who was a friend to everyone.

"The guy was more than physically and athletically gifted," Harrigan notes. "Even when he was a kid in high school, his presence would lift things whenever he walked into a room.

"I have five boys and a girl, and Ernie would come

over and play with them. He was great with kids. . . . On the team, we'd always have some kid who couldn't put his shoulder pads on right and would get all tangled up. While everyone else would head out for practice, Ernie would go over to help him. I can't think of anything more to show the kind of kid he was."

Surprisingly, the one thing Ernie Davis could not do was swim. On a high school all-star outing, the players went picnicking at a nearby lake. Ernie got into water over his head and started thrashing about. He started screaming for help, but his friends thought he was joking. After drinking a good part of the lake, he was finally pulled to safety.

Ernie made All-American his last year in high school and he had college scouts from across the country raving. Everyone wanted to add this "horse" to their backfield.

"I must have made twenty trips down to Elmira that year," recalls Ben Schwartzwalder. "Jim Brown [who graduated from Syracuse University in 1956] went down to the Mark Twain Hotel in Elmira and told Ernie to come to Syracuse. Then they began to correspond. Later, Ernie helped us recruit Floyd [Little]. I think Tony DeFilippo was the big factor though."

Anthony DeFilippo, an Elmira attorney and Syracuse alumnus, had known Ernie since he was in grammar school: his son, Ted, had played end on the same Elmira teams Ernie had starred for. Four years later, DeFilippo would handle Davis' negotiations with the Cleveland Browns.

"There was really no question about him going anywhere but Syracuse University," DeFilippo says. "Ernie was tremendous in high school and he could have gone anywhere. I think following in Jim Brown's footsteps at Syracuse was an important consideration."

For a while, Davis toyed with the idea of attending Notre Dame. He wanted to play for a school with a top-notch schedule and he knew the Fighting Irish's excellence in football. Notre Dame was in South Bend, Indiana, however, and Syracuse was only ninety miles away.

"I had a lot of people talking to me," Ernie said, well after his decision had been made. "But I guess they knew from the start where I was going. Once I thought I would like to go to Notre Dame, but I figured I might get lost in the shuffle. Syracuse is close to home."

Even before Ernie had had time to get acquainted with the Syracuse University campus, the local newspaper was already touting him as the next Jimmy Brown. By then, Brown was scoring touchdowns with the Cleveland Browns. Coach Schwartzwalder made it no easier— he gave Ernie jersey No. 44, the same one Brown had worn.

"He may have felt the pressure," Schwartzwalder says, "but he never showed it. He was always so effervescent, never solemn."

Like Brown, Ernie was big and fast. Brown played at 220 pounds and ran the hundred-yard dash in a very respectable 9.6 seconds; Ernie weighed about 212 pounds and was just as quick. The personalities of the two men, however, were not even remotely alike.

"While Ernie was always so full of enthusiasm," says

144

Schwartzwalder, "Jim always kept to himself. He wasn't outgoing. Ernie loved everyone."

As a sophomore in 1959, Davis walked onto a Syracuse University team that was loaded with talent. The previous year, when Ernie had been a freshman and ineligible for varsity play, the team had made it all the way to the Orange Bowl before losing 20–6 to Oklahoma University. Returning from the same squad this year was the experienced front line led by Roger Davis, Maury Youmans, Bruce Tarbox, Fred Mautino and Bob Yates. All of these men later played professional football.

The backfield, however, was dominated by youth. The lone senior was Ger Schwedes, the captain and right halfback, and with him was Art Baker at fullback, Dave Sarette and Dick Easterly alternating at quarterback— and Ernie Davis at left halfback.

"It was a loose team that produced," recalls Joe Szombathy, now the assistant to the athletic director at Syracuse, and then the offensive and defensive end coach. Yet there were still some early season problems. "We became more cohesive later," says Szombathy, "but I remember after a pregame scrimmage leaving the field with our heads bowed. Our third stringers had just raced through our first team like water through a sieve. We had Kansas coming up and we were a little worried. But we made a few personnel changes, a few coaching moves and it all just jelled."

Football forecasters in 1959 predicted a battle for supremacy in the East between Syracuse, Navy and Penn

State. For many, however, it didn't matter much. Eastern football had been in a downward swing for years; not since the glory years of Doc Blanchard and Glenn Davis at Army in 1944–46 had it been on a par with schools from the Big Ten, Pacific Eight, Atlantic Coast and Southern conferences.

In addition, Syracuse had yet to win a bowl game. Besides the 1958 trouncing by Oklahoma, Syracuse had been invited to only two bowl contests before, losing badly to Alabama in the 1952 Orange Bowl, 61–6, and bowing to Texas Christian University, 28–27, in the 1957 Cotton Bowl.

There was also the question of depth both in the veteran front line and in the relatively untried backfield. Two-platoon football had not yet been introduced in 1959, and the same eleven played both on offense and defense until they petered out and the second string replaced them.

On a warm, clear day at Archibold Stadium, Syracuse University opened its season and Ernie Davis played his first game as a varsity football player. The opponents were the Kansas University Jayhawkers, another good, young team led by a scrappy sophomore quarterback named John Hadl and running back Curtis McClinton, both of whom would later gain a measure of stardom in the pro ranks.

Before more than twenty thousand Syracuse rooters, the Syracuse Orangemen triumphed behind the strength of their running backs, 35–21—and Ernie Davis was on his way. The next week, they were even more impressive, crushing the University of Maryland, 29–0, moving Lincoln Werden of the *New York Times* to call the game "one of Syracuse's greatest modern football performances."

On offense, Syracuse outgained Maryland, 338 yards to 29. "The Sizeable Seven," the nickname given to SU's front line—which was then considered huge at an average size of six feet three inches and 216 pounds—never let the host team get beyond its own thirty-six-yard line. Ernie himself gained seventy-seven yards on the ground—on one run breaking through the Maryland line and running twenty-eight yards for a touchdown—and was named the Most Valuable Player in the game.

Good as these performances were, however, the real turning point for Syracuse came the following week in a driving rain at Annapolis. Navy was led by its sensational halfback, Joc Bellino, who would precede Davis as the Heisman Trophy winner in 1960, and a win by Navy would severely damage Syracuse's chances for the Eastern crown. The Midshipmen, however, were swamped, 32–6. On their very first possession the Orangemen marched downfield for a touchdown, and the game was out of sight thereafter. Ben Schwartzwalder's Wing-T offense, with unbalanced spacings in the line either to the left or right, left Navy completely stymied.

Next came Holy Cross, a true grudge match. Holy Cross had been the only school to beat Syracuse in 1958 —and in 1957—and Syracuse was determined to get its revenge. It did. In the first five minutes of the second period, Syracuse scored three touchdowns, including one on a forty-yard Ernie Davis touchdown run, to pile up a 20–6 lead on its way to a 42–6 runaway.

West Virginia was the same story. Ernie ran wild in perhaps his finest game of the year, gliding in, over and around the defense for 141 yards in just nine carries, including touchdown runs of twenty-nine and fifty-seven yards for a 44–0 victory. Pittsburgh was next, 35–0. The only remaining major obstacle in Syracuse's way was Penn State.

While the Orangemen still had three games left in their schedule, the battle with the Nittany Lions would likely decide: (a) the winner of the Lambert Trophy, given to the top team in the East; (b) a major bowl bid; and (c) a shot at the national championship. Syracuse's record was 6–0, but Penn State's was 7–0, including convincing victories over Army, Illinois and Missouri. The team also boasted two genuine stars in All-American quarterback Richie Lucas and sophomore phenomenon, Roger Kochman, a fast, agile halfback. All of Syracuse's triumphs would be for nothing if they blew this one.

On game day, Syracuse dominated from the outset, breathed a sigh of relief, and then sat back to enjoy its lead—a nearly fatal mistake. Eating up yardage with ease through the first three quarters, the Orangemen took a 20–6 lead on short touchdown runs by Ger Schwedes and Ernie Davis and a short TD pass from Dave Sarette to Dave Baker.

At the beginning of the fourth period, however, the momentum shifted when the eighteen-year-old Kochman received a kickoff at his own goal line and sprinted past the entire Syracuse defense on his way to a one-hundred-yard touchdown. Minutes later, a Syracuse punt was

148

blocked and recovered by Penn State at the Orange one-yard line. A quick plunge later made the score 20–18.

There was 5:25 remaining on the clock, and an aroused Nittany Lion squad knocking on the door; Syracuse had possession, but couldn't afford to give it up. One mistake and the game could be over. So for five minutes and twenty-five seconds, from deep within their own territory, Davis, Schwedes and Baker marched the ball downfield, making one first down after another, and when the whistle blew, the final score read: Syracuse 20, Penn State 18.

The rest of the season was a formality as Syracuse demolished Colgate, 71–0—and immediately afterwards accepted a bid to play in the Cotton Bowl—and then disposed of Boston University, 46–0 (three touchdowns for Ernie), and UCLA, 36–8. For the whole season, Syracuse had amassed a grand total of 273 points and allowed its opponents only 59, a staggering accomplishment. The cynics had been answered.

On New Year's Day, No. 1–ranked Syracuse, the nation's only major undefeated team, came into the Cotton Bowl a two-touchdown favorite to beat fifth-rated Texas, a team that had lost only once to TCU. Right up to game time, however, it was doubtful that Ernie Davis would be able to play because of a muscle pull.

"I'd been worried about him for a week," Schwartz-walder later told reporters. "Ever since he pulled up lame in practice we honestly didn't know if he'd be able to go. And even when he was ready to start, we didn't know how long he'd last."

149

This was the Cotton Bowl, though, and Ernie was not about to be sidelined by a sore leg. In high school, similar aches and pains in his heavily muscled calves had caused him to be taken out of games, but he had always started them. And when he was forced to leave this game in the fourth period with cramps in both legs, he had again made his contribution.

In fact, it was Ernie who nearly beat Texas singlehandedly. On the third play from scrimmage, he pulled in a halfback option pass from Ger Schwedes and raced eighty-seven yards for the opening touchdown in Syracuse's victory. He scored a second touchdown on a twenty-two-yard run, and set up a third with a pass interception. To top it all, he caught a pair of two-point conversion passes from Dave Sarette. Syracuse won, 23–14, and Ernie was named the game's Most Valuable Player.

While it was a magnificent line, and the leadership and maturity of seniors like Ger Schwedes, that took Syracuse University to the top in college football that year, it was Ernie Davis, said his coaches, "who turned the team around."

"He was a leader even as a sophomore," Joe Szombathy says. "He led by his actions on the field, more than by anything he might have said. He did so many things that others couldn't do."

Ernie was just hitting his stride, though. A year later, on a team that would go a "disappointing" 7–2, Davis made one wire service's All-America team and was called by his coach, "the best back in the country."

By this time, the debate over who was the better running back, Ernie Davis or Jimmy Brown, was in full force not only in Syracuse, but throughout the country. In 1958, when Ernie had first arrived at Syracuse, he had told reporters, "I know one thing: I am not another Jim Brown. I'm not that good." Yet to many it appeared that he was exactly that good. Over the years, Ben Schwartzwalder has steadfastly refused to rate his backs, except to say, "I had four great ones." The Davis-Brown debate, of course, was later extended to include Syracuse backs Floyd Little and Larry Csonka.

Before Davis' third year on the Syracuse varsity, however, Stanley Woodward, sports editor for the old New York *Herald Tribune*, met the issue head-on and gave Ernie the edge.

"Davis has abilities that Brown never showed as a college player," wrote Woodward. "Brown didn't block, but Davis does. Brown was not much of a pass receiver. Davis is superb. Brown could pass a little. Davis is better. Brown was a fierce, stamping runner—practically all power; Davis has power but he can streak his way through a broken field and use casual blockers. Brown was a fair defensive man; Davis is a good one."

Davis undeniably was also a much better influence on the rest of the team. While Brown had problems with the coaches and had few friends on the squad, both coaches and teammates were close to Davis.

"I can remember him throwing his arms around Davey Sarette [a white player]," says Schwartzwalder. "Black or white didn't make a difference to him. He was like a puppy dog, always patting guys on the back.

"He roomed with John Mackey [who was a year be-

151

hind him] at Sadler Dorm, but he was close to everyone. The only people who disliked him were the grounds-keepers. If he had anyone to throw a pass to or hold the ball for him—since he liked to kick extra points—he'd stay out there until the lights went out."

Ernie's finest year at Syracuse was as a junior, when he teamed up in the backfield with Mackey, later an all-pro with the Baltimore Colts, and Art Baker, who went on to star with the Hamilton Cats in the Canadian Football League. Though the season ended 7–2, after losses to Pittsburgh and Army, and Syracuse was ignored for a bowl bid, Ernie led the team in rushing for the second straight year and was the third highest ground gainer in the nation. He ran for 877 yards, or 7.7 yards each time he got his hands on the ball, and gained more than a hundred yards rushing in six different games, including a grand total of 130 yards against Miami.

And if that wasn't enough, Ernie decided to play basketball that winter.

In the early 1960s, Syracuse was hardly known for its basketball—in fact, the two went together like oil and water—until Davis and his two football buddies, John Mackey and Don King, reported to Coach Marc Guley.

Davis had played freshman basketball at Syracuse, after his brilliant high school career, but could not play as a sophomore because of the Cotton Bowl. At six feet three inches and a trimmed down 205, though, he still had a sweet shooting touch, a hard drive to the basket and good jumping ability. Ernie moved immediately into the backcourt and made the Orangemen a little more respectable (their record at the time was 2–12). He was instrumental in Syracuse's upset of Penn State by scoring twenty-one points; scored fifteen points against Colgate, LaSalle and Canisius; and in the Canisius game snared eighteen rebounds.

"You just don't stay away from basketball like Ernie has and move right back without feeling the effects," Guley told a reporter before a game against Manhattan College at Madison Square Garden. "You've got to get your shooting touch back and you've got to condition different muscles. But Ernie has that terrific desire. He's simply a great athlete."

Football, however, was first on Ernie's mind, and in the fall of 1961 he was in prime shape for his final season at Syracuse University. Ben Schwartzwalder again fielded a superior team that year—perhaps by the end of the season the strongest team in the East—but luck was not on his side.

After running through Oregon State and West Virginia, Syracuse was sideswiped by a solid Maryland team, 22–21. Two games later Syracuse was stopped again, 14–0, this time by Penn State in its first win over Ernie Davis. Finally, after topping Holy Cross, Pittsburgh and Colgate, it was time for the big one of the season: Notre Dame, the first meeting between the two schools since 1914.

The tradition of the Fighting Irish had always appealed to Ernie. He knew about the fabled Four Horsemen and Knute Rockne's fire-and-brimstone locker room talks and the legend of George Gipp and winning one "for the Gipper." As noted before, he had even considered attending Notre Dame. Now a packed stadium in South Bend had come to see him.

This time, however, Ernie's role was to be a decoy. Every time Davis went into motion or faked into the line, the Notre Dame defense reacted, leaving holes for the other Syracuse runners. Ernie even wore lineman shoulder pads to protect against the expected pounding. All afternoon, Sarette faked handoffs and passes to Ernie while the other men slipped by, and as a result, when the clock ticked down to its final seconds, the score showed Syracuse on top, 15–14.

Many Syracuse supporters still consider this the final score. With three seconds left, Notre Dame attempted a seemingly futile fifty-one-yard field goal; the kick was blocked and thousands of Notre Dame supporters started to look for the exits. But then it happened. A referee threw a penalty flag on the play: Syracuse, roughing the kicker, penalty ten yards. With no time left on the clock, the Notre Dame placekicker received a second life from forty-one yards out. He made the kick—and Syracuse was beaten, 17–15.

It was a bitter loss for Syracuse, even though they won the following Saturday, 28–13 over Boston College, to end the regular season. Ernie ran for ninety-nine yards in twenty carries in that game. Their 7–3 record, with an asterisk in the school program alongside the Notre Dame game, was not particularly illustrious, but it was good enough to get them invited to meet the Miami University Hurricanes in the Liberty Bowl.

There were weeks to go before that final game, however. Much was to happen to Ernie Davis before then.

On November 28, the panel of writers that make up the Heisman committee named Ernie the twenty-seventh winner of the prestigious Heisman Trophy—first won by Jay Berwanger of the University of Chicago in 1935 —and the first black athlete ever to be so honored. Ernie became the third player from the East to win the Heisman in four years, after Pete Dawkins, the Rhodes Scholar from West Point in 1958, and his servicemate, Joe Bellino, from Navy in 1960. Before this sudden eminence, it would have been necessary to go back to Glenn Davis of Army in 1946 to find an Eastern winner.

In the actual tabulation, which is often decided as much by politics and personality as performance, Ernie proved to be the top vote-getter in the East and the third choice throughout the rest of the nation. He accumulated 824 total points to 771 for Bob Ferguson, the powerful but slow Ohio State fullback, 551 for Jimmy Sexton, the diminutive Texas halfback, and 543 for Sandy Stephens, the quarterback from the University of Minnesota and Ernie's old Uniontown friend.

With his mother, stepfather and football coach proudly looking on, Ernie accepted the trophy at a December 6 luncheon at the Downtown Athletic Club in New York City. The question on everybody's mind that day was where Ernie would be playing professional football. Just three days before, Ernie had been the first selection in the college draft, ahead of such players as Roman Gabriel, Merlin Olsen and Bob Ferguson, by both the Washington Redskins of the established National Football League and the Buffalo Bills of the still fledgling American Football League.

"Where I will play, I don't know," he told reporters in the large dining hall. "But I can tell you freely that I'm looking forward to eight or ten years in the professional game."

The AFL needed him badly, as the one big drawing card that would give it some credibility. At the time, they had the big-money owners, but the players were mostly retreads and second echelon. Not until three years later would they get that big star that would guarantee their survival—a quarterback from Alabama named Joe Willie Namath.

"Davis is an exciting player," said Harry Wismer, the owner of the New York Titans [later Jets] in 1961. "It will be good for our league to have him. I believe Ralph Wilson [owner of the Buffalo Bills] will pay him well enough to keep him in our league."

Meanwhile, there had been some bartering going on in the NFL. It was rumored—and later substantiated— that the last-place Redskins had dealt Ernie before the draft to the Browns for Bobby Mitchell, a promising player who would become an all-pro flanker back, and Leroy Jackson, a rookie halfback.

On the day of the Heisman Trophy ceremony, however, such talk was still hearsay. What the reporters wanted to know was if Davis wanted any part of the Redskins. As late as 1961, Washington still had an all-white team because its owner, George Preston Marshall, had refused to sign black players.

156

"I've never had any trouble getting along with people," Ernie told the reporters. "Actually, I've never given any thought to the racial issue."

One reporter asked Ernie how he felt about erasing ten of Jimmy Brown's marks from the Syracuse record book. Davis had set new records in the three major categories: rushing, total yardage and scoring.

"I never thought of breaking Brown's records this year," Ernie said. "Maybe fifteen years or so from now, I'll look back and feel proud of the accomplishment."

A marked man for all defensive teams in 1961, Davis had still managed to run for 823 yards in 150 carries, for an average of 5.5 yards per carry; scored fifteen touchdowns; and pulled in sixteen receptions for 157 yards. With these figures, his career total stood at 2,386 yards rushing to 2,091 for Brown. He had outscored the man who helped recruit him, 220–187. Ernie's total yardage in all departments: 3,414. He had scored thirty-five touchdowns.

His career rushing record, too, would go the way of time. Today, Larry Csonka holds the Syracuse rushing mark with 2,934 yards, followed by Floyd Little at 2,704. Davis, however, still holds the career yards-per-carry mark, often considered the most important record for showing consistency in a ball carrier, with 6.6.

The Heisman Trophy was a major event in his life, but not the only honor Ernie received that December day. President John F. Kennedy happened to be in New York City at the time, and he had made arrangements the previous night to congratulate Ernie in person at the Carlyle

Hotel. A photograph session had run late, however, and the football star missed the President by minutes.

But all was not lost. No sooner had Ernie sat down to the Hall of Fame luncheon, when word came to him that Kennedy would like to see him at the Waldorf Hotel. Since you don't keep a President waiting, Ernie immediately hustled uptown for the appointment, skipping the roast chicken. He made it to the Park Avenue hotel just in time to chat briefly with the Chief Executive. Kennedy, a touch football player of some note and an avid spectator, asked Ernie about his future, but wisely sidestepped the issue of where Ernie would play.

Later that day, Ernie told reporters he had just experienced his two biggest thrills. "First," he said, "is to receive the Heisman award, which I accept not as an individual but as a member of the Syracuse team. The second is that the President wished to meet me."

Ten days later, Ernie and his Syracuse teammates were in Philadelphia for their Liberty Bowl date with Miami, Ernie seemingly unruffled by all the attention being showered on him. "All this is no chore to me," he said to a reporter. "I enjoy it. I know it's only going to happen once."

Davis never stopped smiling and signing autographs that weekend. The questions never fazed him. "I remember a young girl went up to ask Ernie for an autograph," recalls Tony DeFilippo. "He signed it, and then he thanked her for asking for it."

One newspaperman, seeing Davis for the first time, wrote, "He must smile in his sleep. It is the half-surprised, amused, secret smile of a man aware that something immensely pleasurable will happen to him."

It was only twenty-two degrees at game time and only about sixteen thousand fans showed up to see Ernie Davis in his final appearance in the blue and orange of Syracuse University. It was a game that no football fan should have missed.

During the first half, Syracuse looked like a team that had been partying instead of practicing for two weeks. Miami jumped to a 14–0 lead behind the quarterbacking of All-American George Mira.

"We were depressed at halftime," remembers assistant coach Joe Szombathy. "Then Ernie got up and said he would start doing his job in the second half. This revved the whole team up."

After being held to thirty-eight yards in the first half on ten carries, Ernie worked overtime after the intermission. Lugging the ball on what seemed like every down, Davis carried twenty times in the second half alone, for 102 tough yards. Later, in the locker room, he said, "I could have carried the ball twenty times more if it had been necessary."

Ernie had squirmed through the Miami defense for the first Syracuse touchdown on a short run to close the gap, then gained twenty-four yards on four consecutive carries, and acted as a decoy on a handoff up the middle. While half the Miami squad had converged on Ernie, Sarette had rolled out of the pocket and thrown a seven-yard scoring toss to Dick Easterly, wide open in the end zone. The extra point had given Syracuse the lead, and at the whistle, the score had stood Syracuse, 15–14.

His career at Syracuse was over, but his professional fortunes seemed set when, on December 29, 1961, he signed a hefty contract with the Cleveland Browns.

The Browns had been at the very top of the NFL's Eastern division in the mid-1950s, winning titles in 1953, '54 and '57. Lately, however, they had slipped a notch. With Jimmy Brown on the team and Ernie available, they saw the perfect opportunity to go to the formula that Vince Lombardi at Green Bay had transformed into a pair of league championships: deploy two big backs and let them rip.

The Browns, however, still had to sweeten the pot enough to pry Ernie away from the Buffalo Bills. The Bills, it seemed, were willing to put the city in hock for his services. Art Modell, the owner of the Browns, was in a less than enviable bargaining position. Having just traded away one of the finest young players in the game in Bobby Mitchell, he knew he would be in a lot of trouble if he lost Ernie to the AFL.

Taking time off from practicing with the East squad for the annual East-West Shrine Game, Ernie flew to Cleveland to confer with Modell and Tony DeFilippo, who was representing him, with all of sixteen cents in his pocket. One handshake with the Browns' owner and he was the highest-paid rookie in National Football League history.

"Ernie wanted to play with the best competition," DeFilippo says. "He gave up $50,000 by not signing with Buffalo." Davis still managed to walk away from the table that day with an unheard-of sum for the time— $65,000 for the 1962 season and a $15,000 bonus.

Ernie spent a good part of his final college winter in an airplane, traveling from banquet to banquet. From Monday to Friday, he would attend classes—he was an economics major and a solid C student—study, and socialize with his girl friend, Helen Gott, and his football buddies. Then he would pack a suitcase and head off to the Midwest or the South or New England to speak at another dinner and pick up another trophy.

Ernie had a hard time saying no, but his frenetic schedule finally seemed to make him so fatigued that he put his foot down. After all, he had to get in shape for the All-American Bowl Game in Buffalo at the end of June, the Browns' summer camp which started July 8 and the All-Star camp scheduled to open three weeks later.

Before leaving Syracuse, however, he received one final honor. Syracuse had a tradition that the senior who had contributed the most, both athletically and scholastically, to the university led the march of graduating seniors. Ernie was chosen by his classmates to lead the graduation parade. Ernie basked in the honor.

The All-American Game was a disappointment for Ernie, even though the East won, 13–8. Roman Gabriel and Bob Ferguson were the stars of the game, and Ernie was used primarily only as a blocking back.

Marty Harrigan, his high school coach, was in the stands that day to see the final football game Ernie Davis would ever play. "He looked tired then," says Harrigan. "You didn't think of it at the time, but in retrospect it would seem that it [the leukemia] might have already started to affect him. We went to a picnic later, and he

161

ate hot dogs and drank about six bottles of pop, but his gums were bleeding."

Meanwhile, Cleveland Brown coach Paul Brown and owner Modell were busy considering all the possibilities that having the two boys from Syracuse in the same backfield would present. Having discarded veteran quarterback Milt Plum and picked up young Frank Ryan during the off-season, the Browns were optimistic that the team's new look would help them improve upon their 8–5–1 mark in 1961. The fans in Cleveland had every right to think the Browns would challenge the New York Giants and the Pittsburgh Steelers for the title.

"The two of them in the same backfield would have been really something," says Schwartzwalder. "Ernie didn't have Jim's moves, but he was a very hard, fast runner." Szombathy agrees: "With Brown and Davis in the same backfield, you'd have had two runners who could run both inside and outside and catch the ball."

The Syracuse coaches ran an annual summer clinic in Ohio near the Browns' training camp, and that summer in particular they kept popping in to see their two star pupils. Ernie seemed all right, but did not arrive in top shape for the All-Star camp in Evanston, Illinois. He seemed tired and he was having problems with his wisdom teeth. The teeth were finally pulled, which is always a painful and enervating procedure, and he was forced to sit out the first three days of practice.

A week before the game with the champion Packers, with his mouth still sore, Ernie participated in a scrimmage with the Chicago Bears, but on Tuesday, three days before the game, he woke up to find one whole side of his face looking like a balloon. He thought it was due to the recently pulled teeth. A blood test revealed something else, however—monocytic leukemia, the most virulent form of cancer.

Ernie lost his composure for the first and only time, crying when the doctors told him he couldn't play in the College All-Star game. All he was told was that he had a blood disorder, and he guessed it was mononucleosis.

"It's the first big game I've missed in thirteen years," Davis told reporters. "I'll be watching it on television, but it will be rough."

The Packers, who had shut out the Giants in the 1961 title game 37–0, ended up having a tougher time of it with the All-Stars, winning, but by the smaller margin of 42–20. After the game, Lombardi presented Ernie with the game ball.

On August 9, the Browns held an off-the-record press conference and told reporters that Ernie Davis had six to twelve months to live. At the time, Ernie still did not know the extent of his illness, and Brown officials pointed out to the press that it was imperative that no word of it get out.

Ernie stayed in Marymount Hospital in Cleveland for several weeks, still unaware of the gravity of his illness. He felt good and he was without pain, and he could not understand why he was not out practicing with the Browns.

"What I remember most from last summer," he later wrote in a magazine article for *The Saturday Evening Post*, "is waking up early in the morning and staring at hospital walls. There was nothing to do except think.

At first, that was the worst part of it. It was a very lonely time."

Soon after his illness had been diagnosed, the Syracuse University coaches went to see Ernie, but before they could go into his room, a nurse told Schwartzwalder to make the most of the visit—he would never see Ernie alive again. The coach later believed that Ernie sensed this, too.

"When we got up to leave," Schwartzwalder remembers, "he said, 'You can't leave because I'll never see you again.' You can't imagine what this did to us."

Tony DeFilippo came to Marymount with an Elmira internist in tow. A doctor at the hospital showed them the slides with Ernie's blood and explained to them that it was hopeless. DeFilippo decided to play a long shot. He took Ernie out of the hospital in Cleveland and moved him to the National Institutes of Health in Bethesda, Maryland, for special treatment.

"He was still a very sick boy," DeFilippo recalls, "and we went through the back door of the hospital so no one would see us. [At Bethesda] he was given the drug and the remission set in."

"The drug" was called six-mercaptopurine, or simply 6-MP, and it did indeed induce a temporary remission of Ernie's condition. Within a matter of weeks, Ernie's blood count became normal, the swelling in his face and neck went down and he felt better. He even felt good enough to attend an exhibition doubleheader in Cleveland on August 18. When his name came over the loudspeaker, a sellout crowd of 77,683 fans rose to their feet and gave Davis a five-minute ovation.

It was not until October 4 that Ernie at last became fully aware of his condition. All he had known was that he was seriously ill. Others seemed to know more than he did. Once, standing outside a movie theater in downtown Cleveland, a stranger came up to him and asked, "Are you Ernie Davis?" Not wishing to make a fuss, Ernie said he was not. Then the man said, "You're lucky you're not. Ernie Davis has leukemia; he won't live six months."

Ernie turned and walked away. There was really nothing he could say.

Meanwhile, there was a battle underway between his advisor, his boss and the doctors. DeFilippo, for one, did not want Ernie to be burdened with the knowledge of his disease. Ernie himself had never asked the doctors about his illness, because, as he later said, "I was afraid of what the answer would be." He must have had suspicions, though. Once, driving back from Bethesda with Tony DeFilippo and Art Modell, a book inadvertently fell out of Ernie's pocket. It dealt with death and burial.

Finally, on a warm day in Cleveland, Dr. Austin Weisberger, a well-respected hematologist and the physician who had been treating Ernie, called him into his office. Also in the room was Dr. Vic Ippolito, the Browns' team physician.

"Ernie," said Dr. Weisberger, "we think you're ready to be told what your illness is."

He had leukemia, the doctor told him, but there was also good news: he was now in a perfect state of remission. There was a chance he could live a long and normal life. Consequently, Dr. Weisberger said, there was no reason why he could not begin working out with the Browns again.

"He was confused, of course, when we told him," Modell later told reporters. "He was relieved to find out what the trouble actually had been. But he's gratified that he can play football again. He wants to play so badly."

That was true. Ernie had felt fine for weeks and had been climbing the walls for a chance to play football. Now aware of what all the tests and medication and blood therapy had meant—if still not sure whether or not he had beaten the disease—his spirits soared.

"I felt almost free and easy," he wrote. "It was as if something that had been pressing down on me for weeks had suddenly been lifted."

Under the direction of Dr. Ippolito, Ernie immediately began a conditioning program. While his teammates prepared for the following Sunday's game, Ernie did situps and pushups and jumping jacks. He ran sprints and underwent stamina drills. There were eleven games remaining in the Browns' 1962 season, and Ernie figured he could still be a part of it.

The Browns' management was divided, however, over whether Ernie should be permitted to play. As the season neared completion, it became apparent that the Browns were not going anywhere in the standings. The Giants had run away with the division and only the Steelers were within hailing distance. The Browns were mired in third place (where they eventually finished with a 7–6–1 record).

166

A national debate of sorts took place. Should a man suffering from a possibly fatal disease be allowed to climb into a uniform and play professional football? Medical opinion was sought, received and published in newspapers all over the country.

"He should be in as good shape as ever as long as the remission lasts," said Dr. Charles Dean of the Ohio State University Medical School, who suggested Davis be allowed to play.

"I doubt very seriously he would be one hundred percent and I doubt whether it would be fair to his teammates or even to opposing players, let alone to him," said Dr. James Grace of the Roswell Park Memorial Hospital in Buffalo. Although Dr. Grace believed those in remission could and should live normal lives, he thought Ernie's was an extreme case. "This is hard, tough, professional football. The more I think of it, the more ridiculous it seems."

A third doctor, Dr. Sidney Farber of Children's Hospital in Boston, took still another side. He thought Ernie should work out with the team, and then let the team make the decision. He added, though, that Ernie's most valuable contribution would probably be as an advisor or assistant coach. "How much rough-and-tumble can be taken is a question," said Dr. Farber. "We don't advise fisticuffs or football for our patients in remission, but I suppose if I had leukemia, I would try to live life to the hilt."

Paul Brown, the Cleveland head coach (and the man for whom the team is named), did not think Ernie be-

167

longed on the football field, at least not that year. Although the doctors and front office seemed to favor it, Brown said no.

Later that winter, after the season was over, Modell fired Paul Brown and hired an assistant coach with the Browns, Blanton Collier, as his replacement. There were many writers and fans who believed Brown was released because he refused to play Ernie. At the time, though, Ernie was obviously disappointed, but did not argue with Brown's decision. "This is when it gets really frustrating," he said. "I'm in real good shape, but it's too late in the season to work me into the setup."

Ernie was still optimistic, though. "Starting next year," he told the press, "I expect to play ten or eleven years and then go into business. I'd like to get into purchasing or marketing, something where I could use what I learned in college."

Ernie spent the final part of the season sitting on the bench in civilian clothes—he never did get to wear his uniform No. 45—and surprising his teammates with his football knowledge. He could pick out the strong points and weaknesses of his opponents and teammates, pointing out how one player made up in experience and common sense what he lacked in speed or quickness, and how another player looked good in certain situations but could be attacked successfully in others. He refused to feel sorry for himself. After all, he still had his plans.

In March, 1963, Ernie was still thinking of playing football with the Browns. "The best thing to me in football has always been the competitiveness," he wrote in a magazine article. "Sometimes when the game is close and the play is roughest you forget the crowd and the noise, and it is just you against somebody else to see who is the better man. That is what I like and took pride in the way I could do it and, after all the waiting, I want a chance to do it again."

The article was not completely optimistic, however. There was every reason to think that Ernie Davis was also writing a eulogy to himself, to a man who knew he was dying.

"Some people say I'm unlucky," wrote Davis. "I don't believe it. And I don't want to sound as if I am particularly brave or unusual. Sometimes I still get down and sometimes I feel sorry for myself.

"In these years I have had more than most people get in a lifetime. I think everyone wants some kind of recognition. Something that will pick them out of a crowd and make people admire them."

That winter Ernie worked as a salesman with the Pepsi Cola Co. and did film studies for the Browns.

"There was hope after the season that he would make it," wrote Jimmy Brown in his autobiography, *Off My Chest.* "He ran longer and harder than the rest. He bowled and played golf. He played like a tiger with the [Browns] basketball team."

Davis and Brown often shopped for clothes and went to parties together. Ernie had conservative tastes in clothes, opting for Ivy League or old English cuts.

In February, Ernie fell out of remission and had to stop playing basketball. He needed immediate blood transfusions and medication. However, he never talked to his teammates, coaches or friends about his illness or

169

about his fears. Once when his roommate John Brown was discoursing on the uncertainties and insecurities of life, Ernie said softly, "I may not make it, John, but that doesn't mean I have to quit trying."

Although he was like a son to Marty Harrigan, his old coach at Elmira Free Academy, he never burdened him with his feelings either. "I spoke to Ernie two weeks before his death," Harrigan says. "He never talked about it to me. All he said was that, 'We'll get some money and invest it.' "

Tony DeFilippo never heard a word of bitterness or self-pity from Davis. "I think Ernie suspected he was dying and he took it pretty well," DeFilippo says. "You never knew of course what was going on inside of him. He was just the greatest gentleman in the world. You could not find a finer person."

Ben Schwartzwalder and Joe Szombathy saw Ernie one final time in Syracuse. It was at the annual spring varsity vs. alumni football game and Davis had come to coach the alumni.

"He looked okay, but you could see the swelling," remembers Szombathy. "You wouldn't think he was so ill at the game. He never showed it. He took everything so casually. He was as effervescent as could be."

Jimmy Brown picked up Ernie at his apartment to go to a party that spring. It was a night Brown has never forgotten. "He looked terribly tired," Brown wrote in his autobiography. "I wanted to say, 'Look, Ernie, if you're a little tired or you feel under the weather, why not skip the party.' I wanted to back out of the party,

170

but I knew if I did Ernie would know why. If I had so much as mentioned that he looked tired, it would have been like hitting him in the belly.

"We sat there and talked awhile, all the time I hoped he'd say, 'I'm a little bushed tonight, Jim. I think I'll skip the party.' But of course, he didn't say anything of the kind. While we talked, I noticed, suddenly, that Ernie had a small wad of cotton stuffed into his nose. He had stuffed it well up where it could not easily be seen, but it slipped down. Ernie's hand leaped to his face. He pretended to be idly fingering his nose while he stuffed the cotton back into place. I looked the other way, pretending not to notice. I was sick at heart. Nose bleeds, I knew, were a grave sign. The speck of blood told me it was the beginning of the end."

The week of his death, Brown and Davis were at a card party with some teammates. Ernie's neck had started to swell badly and he appeared in pain. After a while, he got up to leave, saying good-naturedly, "It's not very lively here, I think I'll go home."

On May 16, Ernie paid a final visit to Art Modell and apologized to him for the expense of his medical care. They talked briefly of next season. Ernie told Modell he was confident that the Browns would win the championship in 1963.

At the time, Modell realized how strange it was for Ernie to come in personally to see him. Usually, he telephoned. Not until later, did he realize that this was Ernie's way of saying goodbye.

The next day, Ernie entered Lakeside Hospital in

Cleveland. Soon, he fell into a coma and at 2:00 A.M. on May 18, Ernie Davis died. He was twenty-three years old.

On May 23, sixteen hundred people filled the cemetery at the First Baptist Church in Elmira and more than three thousand stood in the park during a fifteen minute service, to pay their final respects to Ernie. His body lay in state at the Neighborhood House where he had played basketball as a youth.

President Kennedy sent a telegram calling Ernie "an outstanding young man of great character, who consistently served as an inspiration to the young people of this country."

There were other words of praise. Coach Schwartzwalder called Ernie the "perfect athlete. . . . He was talented, dedicated and selfless. He was a wonderful boy who set a fine example for youngsters everywhere."

Syracuse University Chancellor William Tolley said, "He was as fine a man as he was an athlete whether in the classroom or dormitory or on the playing field."

More than a decade and a half later, things have changed in Cleveland, in Syracuse and in Elmira.

Jimmy Brown has left Cleveland and football for Hollywood and the movies. He has made a few good films, and more than a few bad ones. Ernie Davis, Brown said, was the most courageous man he ever met.

"Ernie died the way he wanted to, inconveniencing nobody," Brown wrote. "I know of no greater humility. Ernie Davis was not afraid to die. But he was embarrassed for grieving his friends."

172

The Heisman Trophy from 1961 sits in a glass case in Manley Field House on the Syracuse University campus. At Sadler Dormitory, there is a plaque dedicated to Ernie Davis.

Ben Schwartzwalder has long since turned the coaching reins over to younger men. Football at Syracuse University has never approached the Davis years, and probably never will again. A national ranking, much less a national championship, seems light years away.

The junior high school in the north side of Elmira is now called Ernie Davis Junior High School. The old Elmira Free Academy has been torn down and Ernie Davis Park has replaced it. Tony DeFilippo has brought his sons into the law firm. Ernie's mother has remarried and is now Marie Fleming. She sold the old house on Lake Street and now lives in the south side of the city.

Marty Harrigan has hung up his football cleats and whistle, but is still trying to get young "horses" into college. Today he is the principal of the new Elmira Free Academy. He uses Ernie Davis as an example to other athletes, even though he knows deep down there will never be another Ernie Davis.

"Ernie Davis," he says, "was the greatest thing that ever happened in my life."

Steven Clark, twenty-seven, is a newspaper reporter in New York and the author of *The Complete Book of Baseball Cards* and *Roller Hockey*. A native of Lake Success, New York, and a graduate of Syracuse University, he now lives with his wife Holly in Fort Lee, New Jersey.